Praise for *The Perfect SENCO*

The Perfect SENCO is an absolute 'must' for head teachers and SENCOs. Natalie is highly skilled at explaining the 'big picture' and then providing practical strategies to ensure that what happens in school 'syncs' with national initiatives. If the advice in this book is followed, then schools can be assured that they are Ofsted ready and also that all statutory requirements are met. Included in the book are pro formas that can easily be adapted for each establishment or used as they are.

Each chapter concludes with a 'mini' plenary which is useful to consolidate learning and also to use as a quick reference point.

The Perfect SENCO is a special book: it ensures that it provides up to date advice which incorporates the changing landscape of SEN. It is also educational in that it can be used as a catalyst for school improvement and evaluation, meeting the requirements of Ofsted.

The book takes into consideration the needs of children, their outcomes being the main focus. If teachers and senior leaders implement the strategies, this will provide a co-ordinated approach for school improvement.

I would recommend this book, without reservation, to every school.

Carol Aspinall, Independent Education Consultant

This book is an absolute must read for *all* teachers and school leaders. Well selected accounts of practice and case studies offer insight into the practical aspects of achieving the aim of success for all our children, irrespective of need. There is no doubt that this should be on the reading list of any aspirant teacher who is attempting to discover a moral purpose and personal vision for education. Natalie's wealth of experience of special educational needs strategy, coupled with her huge desire for equality for all children, gives a clear insight into how to develop an educational philosophy whilst enabling opportunities for any teacher to be confident in becoming *The Perfect SENCO*.

Chris Wheatley, Executive Head The Cotgrave Candleby Lane School, C.E.O. Flying High Trust

The Perfect SENCO provides a comprehensive and realistic view of one of the most important teaching roles in our schools today. The current climate of change surrounding the provisions we make in our schools, and settings for children and young people with special educational needs, will lead to an even greater level of significance for the role of the SENCO and the professional development implications to ensure that every teacher is a teacher of every child. As Natalie rightly identifies, achieving perfection is often out of reach for most of us; however, *The Perfect SENCO* offers all of us in education, not just SENCOs, a fantastic, highly readable guide in striving for perfection to ensure that the needs of our most vulnerable pupils and students are fundamental to all schools' philosophy, strategy, planning and practice. Most importantly, the book provides clear routes in determining effective outcomes for children and young people. The top tips, useful summaries, checklists and templates will refresh any SENCO's toolbox, enabling them to keep up-to-date, at the top of their game and meet the challenge of the changing landscape for SEN. This is a must read for every teacher, SENCO, senior leader and school governor.

Jane Friswell, SEND Consultant, Education Development Officer, nasen (National Association of Special Educational Needs)

Never has education seen so much change in such a short period of time, especially with regard to SEND and its coordination. During the coming academic year, and from 2014, schools will need to work differently, leaving behind the medicalised approach to SEND as a deficit model and moving towards a more proactive, whole-school approach. This is something good schools have always done; however, for some a more collaborative, corporate approach will be a significant change. This is, however, essential in order to meet the needs of twenty-first century learners.

Natalie Packer's new book, *The Perfect SENCO*, considers the key tenets of the twenty-first century SENCO, with particular regard to the new ways of working that colleagues will face.

Considering the SENCO role as one centred around school improvement is an important distinction that some colleagues maintaining an approach based upon a medical model will need to understand. This publication tackles this as part of a whole-school approach, considering high quality provision and effective partnerships as key elements of that new way of working.

In addition, clear guidance and support with regard to self-evaluation and inspections helps SENCO colleagues measure and evidence impact; another key facet of the modern SENCO way.

Throughout the book, case studies and examples, along with Top Tips, bring the text to life - these allow the reader an opportunity to understand the context and support a greater depth of understanding. This book is timely for a number of reasons, not only due to the significant changes that lie ahead with regard to provision and assessment of SEND, but also because, at a time of austerity, it allows the reader to see that effective provision does not need to be expensive; a desire to improve outcomes as part of a whole school approach is a key starting point. This, coupled with the themes that run through the book, with regard to collaboration and partnerships, school improvement and evaluation, provide a condensed and cohesive manuscript that should find a valuable home in all SENCO's offices/bookcases.

As an experienced SENCO, who has been fortunate enough to coordinate some high quality outcomes for some of our most vulnerable learners, I can align myself with all the publication's key themes; this is no surprise as good practice has always been one of partnerships and collaboration that is child-centred. As a tool for helping focus experienced SENCOs on key areas, or for the newly appointed; *The Perfect*

SENCO is an ideal companion for the challenges we face; especially in light of the imminent, significant changes in policy and provision.

I have no reservations in wholeheartedly recommending this book to anyone SENCO, teacher, Head teacher, member of support staff, or anyone interested in improving outcomes for our most vulnerable; easy to read and understand, the distillation of what can be extremely complex into clear and explicit areas is a real breath of fresh air in the dense fog of political change.

Gareth D Morewood, Director of Curriculum Support & Specialist Leader of Education, Priestnall School, Honorary Research Fellow, University of Manchester

THE PERFECT
SENCO

Natalie Packer
Edited by Jackie Beere

 Independent Thinking Press

First published by
Independent Thinking Press
Crown Buildings, Bancyfelin, Carmarthen, Wales, SA33 5ND, UK
www.independentthinkingpress.com

Independent Thinking Press is an imprint of Crown House Publishing Ltd.

British Library Cataloguing-in-Publication Data
A catalogue entry for this book is available
from the British Library.

Print ISBN 978-1-78135-104-8
Mobi ISBN 978-1-78135-119-2
ePub ISBN 978-1-78135-120-8

Printed and bound in the UK by
Gomer Press, Llandysul, Ceredigion

I dedicate this book to my partner, Frank, for his patience during my many hours of writing.

Acknowledgements

Thank you to the colleagues who provided me with great examples, tips and case studies to include. Special thanks also to my friend and amazing consultant, Caroline Bentley-Davies, for encouraging me to write the book in the first place.

Contents

Foreword

A school is only as good as the progress of its most vulnerable, challenging child. This has never been more true than now, as Ofsted has increased the pressure on schools to ensure they are meeting the needs of all pupils, especially those with learning challenges. However, funding levels have been cut, so the number of pupils meeting the criteria to attract extra resources and one-to-one support continues to spiral downwards.

Allied to this, the credibility of teaching assistants – the traditional support for needy pupils – is being questioned as research emerges which challenges their effectiveness in helping them to become better learners. The use that schools make of the Pupil Premium to support underprivileged children is also being ruthlessly scrutinised. If interventions to help needy pupils are not delivering results, we can now expect big questions to be asked of the school leadership.

The school special educational needs coordinator (SENCO), who drives the policy and practice that leads to successful outcomes for these special children, has become pivotal to the success of every school. This leadership role, rooted in ensuring that everyday classroom practice caters for vulnerable learners, provides a tough challenge. The work that SENCOs do can only be effective if it is entrenched in the values and vision of a school leadership which puts learning at the heart of its mission, and the SENCO at the heart of its leadership team.

What Natalie Packer has managed to do brilliantly in this book is to provide that vision and framework to help every practising SENCO, or would-be SENCO, understand how to do the very best job for vulnerable children so that they can make progress and close the gap. Closing that gap – between the children who succeed at school and those that, for what-ever reason, struggle to achieve – is the key role of the SENCO and their team. However, this won't be done solely by providing one-to-one support, or nurture groups, or even a team of enthusiastic, retrained teaching assistants. The only way to really help these children to make outstanding progress is through the high expectations of every teacher in every classroom, every hour of every day for 38 weeks of the year. These children may not be getting the type of emotional support that creates resilient learners at home, so school could be the only chance they have.

A SENCO is thus central to the whole-school drive to realise consistently high quality teaching. This includes tracking and engaging pupils so that they can achieve their full potential. At the heart of high quality outcomes for all children is a culture of high expectations and the belief that there *is* a way to help every child achieve more. The SENCO who can drive up expectations and commitment in every lesson and who, therefore, delivers results for the most challenging children, will be much in demand. This book is invaluable because it is full of useful advice and practical strategies that will be used again and again to deliver that vision of outstanding progress for vulnerable children in every classroom.

This book is so good that it should be read not only by SENCOs but by every member of the leadership team, governors and every middle leader. Why? Because in order to deliver for *all* pupils, *all* teachers and leaders need to understand how to find ways to help children with special educational needs to make breakthroughs in learning, gain confidence and achieve the very best results they can.

In uncertain times, with expectations high, one thing is certain – a school is only as good as its SENCO.

Jackie Beere, Tiffield

List of abbreviations

AfL	Assessment for Learning
APS	average points score
ASD	autistic spectrum disorder
ASDAN	Award Scheme Development and Accreditation Network
BESD	behavioural, emotional and social difficulties
CAF	Common Assessment Framework
CAT	Cognitive Abilities Test
CPD	continuing professional development
CUREE	Centre for the Use of Research and Evidence in Education
DCSF	Department for Children, Schools and Families
DfE	Department for Education
DfEE	Department for Education and Employment
DISS	Deployment and Impact of Support Staff
EAL	English as an additional language
EEF	Education Endowment Fund
EHC	Education, Health and Care (plan)

EHRC	Equality and Human Rights Commission
FFT	Fischer Family Trust
ICT	information and communication technology
IDP	Inclusion Development Programme
IEP	individual education plan
LA	local authority
MLD	moderate learning difficulties
NASENCO	National Award for Special Educational Needs Coordinators
NQT	newly qualified teacher
PCP	person-centred planning
PSHE	personal, social, health and economic (education)
QTS	qualified teacher status
RAISE	Reporting and Analysis for Improvement through School Self-Evaluation
SEAL	Social and Emotional Aspects of Learning
SEN	special educational needs
SENCO	special educational needs coordinator
SEND	special educational needs and disabilities
SLCN	speech, language and communication needs
SLT	senior leadership team
TA	teaching assistant
TAC	team around the child

Introduction

> ## Wanted: Special Educational Needs Coordinator (SENCO)
>
> Must be efficient, organised, enthusiastic and flexible.
>
> Must be highly skilled in assessing and meeting the needs of the most vulnerable pupils.
>
> Must be able to motivate and support staff to ensure all pupils make exceptional progress – all day, every day!

Have you ever wondered what it means to be the 'perfect' special educational needs coordinator (SENCO)? For those of you who have been a SENCO for a number of years, in the early days it is likely that your role consisted mainly of working with small groups of pupils and writing mountains of targets. Over recent years, however, the job of the SENCO has become more strategic and will now include provision mapping, working in partnership with parents, supporting other colleagues, commissioning services, demonstrating pupil progress and ensuring value for money. In essence, it is a role which contributes significantly to whole-school improvement.

It has never been easy to give a clear definition that encompasses the vast nature of the SENCO job and, to some extent, it is open to interpretation by the head teacher and governors of individual schools.[1] However, the importance of the role is clear: the SENCO is currently only one of two statutory school roles (the other, of course, is the head teacher). But only one of these roles requires someone with qualified teacher status (QTS) – and it's not the head!

This requirement for all schools to have a qualified SENCO, in addition to the introduction of the National Award for SENCOs (NASENCO), has helped to raise the status of the role significantly. Along with raised status, however, comes increased responsibility and accountability. High quality professional development, support and accurate information are essential if the SENCO is to fulfil their role efficiently and effectively.

It could be argued that, ultimately, the purpose of the SENCO it is to do themselves out of a job. Why? Because a key priority must be to ensure that *all* teachers are fulfilling their responsibilities towards pupils with special educational

---

1   The current regulations concerning SENCOs can be found in DfE (2009), The Education (Special Educational Needs Co-ordinators) (England) (Amendment) Regulations 2009. SI No. 1387. Available at: http://www. legislation.gov.uk/uksi/2009/1387/made?view=plain/ This will be replaced in September 2014 by DfE (2013), The Education (Special Educational Needs Co-ordinator) (England) Regulations 2014. Available at: http://media. education.gov.uk/assets/files/pdf/c/clause%2062%20draft%20regulations%20 sen%20coordinators.pdf (both accessed 17 June 2013).

needs (SEN). Providing support for colleagues in school through training, coaching, mentoring or joint planning will enable all staff to become more confident in their own classroom practice. However, although it should be acknowledged that *every* teacher is a teacher of children with special educational needs, the SENCO is there not only to act as an advocate for these children, but because they are instrumental in developing the whole-school processes and practice upon which inclusive teaching and learning can be built.

The aim of this book is to support those professionals in school who have overall responsibility for ensuring high quality provision for, and progress of, pupils with SEN. Its purpose is to provide guidance for SENCOs on working in a strategic way to support improvement. It will be of use not only for potential or newly appointed SENCOs, but also for those who are more experienced and wish to keep their day-to-day practice up to date.

The book can be used in a number of ways:

- As a point of reference for busy SENCOs.
- For SENCOs to use as part of their own professional development.
- To encourage reflection of current policy and practice.
- To support cultural and systemic change in school.

This book has been published at a time when there is significant change occurring within education, particularly in the world of special educational needs. The implications of the government's *Support and Aspiration* Green Paper[2] is resulting in many challenges for schools, parents and the wide range of services dedicated to improving the life chances of some of our most vulnerable youngsters. September 2012 brought with it the introduction of yet another Ofsted framework,[3] which has an increased focus on judging how well schools provide for pupils with SEN and for those with disabilities. Along with other changes, including the focus on disadvantage through the Pupil Premium, a new funding framework, the 2012 *Teachers' Standards*[4] and a revised curriculum, there is much for school leaders to consider.

However, these changes are also bringing about new opportunities and some schools are looking, for example, to redefine the role of the SENCO. Many are now taking a fully inclusive approach and incorporating responsibility for other vulnerable groups, including looked after children or those eligible for free school meals. No matter which way leaders choose to define the role in their school, ultimately they need

2   DfE (2011), *Support and Aspiration: A New Approach to Special Educational Needs and Disability. A Consultation*. Available at: http://webarchive.nationalarchives. gov.uk/20130401151715/https://www.education.gov.uk/publications/standard/ publicationDetail/Page1/CM%208027 (accessed 17 June 2013).

3   Ofsted (2013), *The Framework for School Inspection 2012*. Ref: 120100. Available at: http://www.ofsted.gov.uk/resources/framework-for-school-inspection (accessed 17 June 2013).

4   DfE (2012), *Teachers' Standards*. Available at: https://www.education.gov.uk/ publications/eOrderingDownload/teachers%20standards.pdf (accessed 17 June 2013).

to ensure that pupils with SEN receive the highest quality provision and make excellent progress.

Getting the role right is not just about ticking boxes for Ofsted or ensuring we are following the latest government message; we do it because we want to make a difference to the lives of children. This may sound clichéd but, in my experience, I have found that SENCOs are some of the most passionate and dedicated staff in our schools and genuinely strive to do the best for their pupils. *The Perfect SENCO* aims to support those professionals to make that difference.

Chapter 1

The SENCO: centre stage for school improvement

'We want to put in place a radically different system to support better life outcomes for young people; give parents confidence by giving them more control; and transfer power to professionals on the front line and to local communities.'[1]

How many new policies, ideas and initiatives have you experienced since you became a teacher or leader? Probably quite a few! From 2014, a number of you will witness the most significant national change in SEN since you became a SENCO (more on this below). Keeping up to date with the latest legislation and guidance is now more important than ever to ensure you can respond to the changes that are occurring. In 2011, the government launched their SEN Green Paper, *Support and Aspiration: A New Approach to Special*

---

1 DfE, *Support and Aspiration: A Consultation*, p. 4.

Educational Needs and Disability. A Consultation. The paper outlined their vision for improving the SEN system so that it works better for young people with special educational needs and their families. The aim is to achieve this through a focus on:

- Securing early identification, assessment and intervention.
- Giving parents more control over, and confidence in, the system.
- Ensuring staff in schools have appropriate skills, knowledge and experience to support pupils with SEN.
- Helping young people with SEN to prepare for adulthood.
- Enabling joint working between education, health and social care.
- Increasing accountability of all services to ensure better outcomes.

In 2012, the government published its response to the consultation on the Green Paper in *Progress and Next Steps*.[2] The Children and Families Bill[3] followed in 2013 to take forward

---

2 DfE (2012), *Support and Aspiration: A New Approach to Special Educational Needs and Disability. Progress and Next Steps*. Available at: http://media.education.gov. uk/assets/files/pdf/s/support%20and%20aspiration%20a%20new%20 approach%20to%20special%20educational%20needs%20and%20disability%20 %20%20progress%20and%20next%20steps.pdf (accessed 17 June 2013).

3 House of Commons (2012), Children and Families Bill 2012–13 to 2013–14. London: HMSO. Available at: http://services.parliament.uk/bills/2012-13/ childrenandfamilies.html (accessed 17 June 2013).

the legislative proposals. Here is a brief summary of the key points:

- Replace statements with a single-assessment process and a combined Education, Health and Care (EHC) plan which will run from birth to 25 years and focus on long-term outcomes.

- Include parents more in the assessment process and hand them control of funding for support of their child's needs through a personal budget.

- Give parents more choice over the school they choose for their child.

- Replace School Action and School Action Plus with a single, school-based SEN support category.

- Improve teacher training and professional development to include more focus on supporting pupils with SEN.

- Require local authorities to produce a summary of the 'local offer' of services available for supporting children with SEN and their families.

- Provide access to quality post-16 vocational and work-related learning options for young people with SEN.

- Encourage voluntary and community sector organisations to contribute to local SEN provision.

- Reduce bureaucracy and introduce a new SEN Code of Practice.

The SEN code of practice

At the time of writing, a draft Code of Practice had been made available providing an indication of some of the implications of the Green Paper for schools and other organisations (the final Code will be published in 2014). *The (0–25) Special Educational Needs Code of Practice*[4] provides statutory guidance and practical advice on how to carry out statutory duties to identify, assess and make provision for children and young people's SEN as set out in the Children and Families Bill. The code also sets out how legislation and regulations concerning children and young people with disabilities works alongside this.

The Code is based upon a number of key principles:

- There is early identification of needs.
- High expectations and aspirations are set for what children and young people with SEN and disabilities (SEND) can achieve.
- There is a focus on the outcomes that children and young people and their families want to achieve.
- The views and participation of children and young people and their parents/carers are central.
- Children and young people and their parents have more control over support.

---

4 DfE (2013), *Indicative Draft: The (0–25) Special Educational Needs Code of Practice*. Available at http://media.education.gov.uk/assets/files/pdf/s/sen%20code%20 of%20practice%20indicative%20draft%20for%20committee.pdf (accessed 17 June 2013).

- Education, health and social care partners collaborate to coordinate support.
- Everyone involved is clear about roles and responsibilities.
- High quality provision is in place to meet needs effectively.
- The skills, knowledge and attitude of those working with children and young people are central to achieving excellent outcomes.

The Children and Families Bill requires local authorities and their partners, including health care providers, to jointly commission services for children and young people with SEN. They must publish information about the provision they expect to be available in their area for those who have SEN. This is known as the 'local offer' and many schools are already looking at how they can develop their own 'school offer' as part of the local package of support.

The Code of Practice highlights the rights of all children and young people to receive an appropriate education, with opportunities to achieve their goals and aspirations. Those pupils who have SEN, and who require support or interventions that are additional to those normally provided as part of the differentiated curriculum, will be given school-based SEN support. This change from School Action and School Action Plus reflects the move to a more coordinated category as part of the school's overall, graduated response to SEN support.

The draft Code identifies the following four main areas of need that characterise pupils with SEN, and where they may require school-based support:

1. Communication and interaction

2. Cognition and learning

3. Emotional, social and behavioural development

4. Sensory and/or physical

For those with complex needs who, despite school-based SEN support, do not make progress, an EHC plan may be appropriate. In 2014, EHC plans will be introduced in England and Wales to offer a coordinated approach to the delivery of services across education, health and care. As integrated support plans, they will be focused on achieving outcomes and helping children and young people to make a positive transition to adulthood, and will be produced in partnership with parents and the young people themselves. Parents of children with an EHC plan will also be given the option of having a personal budget.

These changes will set the climate for SEN over the next few years. This book takes into consideration some of the resulting implications – as far as is possible in a world where change continues to happen at such a rapid pace.

SEN in the Ofsted framework

In addition to changes in the SEN system, there are significant implications for SENCOs in the current Ofsted framework. The September 2012 framework focuses on those aspects that have the most impact on improving outcomes for children and young people.[5] Inspectors make judgements in four key areas:

- The achievement of pupils at the school.
- The quality of teaching in the school.
- The behaviour and safety of pupils at the school.
- The quality of leadership in and management of the school.

At the same time, however, inspectors must also consider the spiritual, moral, social and cultural development of pupils, as well as:

> 'the extent to which the education provided by the school meets the needs of the range of pupils at the school, and in particular the needs of:
>
> - pupils who have a disability for the purposes of the Equality Act 2010
> - pupils who have special educational needs.'[6]

---

5   Ofsted, *Framework for School Inspection 2012*.
6   Ofsted (2013), *School Inspection Handbook*. Ref: 120101, p. 23. Available at http://www.ofsted.gov.uk/resources/school-inspection-handbook (accessed 17 June 2013).

The emphasis is on those pupils who are underachieving and who are not making expected progress. Some of these pupils may have an identified SEN or disability; others may be underachieving because they are simply not receiving the support they need to improve. The key to a school's success is to show they are providing high quality provision to *every* pupil *every* day.

Inspectors will also be keen to see how schools are using their Pupil Premium funding and what the impact has been on improving outcomes for disadvantaged pupils. Some of your pupils with SEN may be benefitting from additional provision through the Pupil Premium and, where this is the case, it is important that you are involved in conversations about the use and impact of the funding.

With this increased emphasis on SEN and other vulnerable groups in the framework, the SENCO has a key part to play in providing evidence to support the judgements the school makes about itself. In order to showcase your school, you will need to be prepared to show evidence that:

- The practice reflects high expectations and high aspirations for pupils with SEN.
- The learning and progress of groups of pupils, particularly those with SEN, show that they achieve exceptionally well.
- Pupils with SEN are making rapid and sustained progress as a result of excellent teaching.

■ The school has successful strategies for engaging with parents, including those who find working with the school difficult.

Chapter 7 provides further advice on how the SENCO can support the whole-school self-evaluation process and prepare for the inspection visit.

Challenges and opportunities

If the thought of keeping up with the national agenda makes you dizzy, don't worry – you're not alone! Change undoubtedly brings with it an element of challenge. Some of the challenges that SENCOs report they are currently facing include:

■ Informing staff and supporting them to manage any school-based changes.

■ Working with parents and families more effectively.

■ The implications of personal budgets on management of provision.

■ Recruitment and deployment of teaching assistants (TAs).

■ Practical implications of working with health and social care.

■ Changes to funding and impact on school budget.

■ Increasing workload.

■ Time (or lack of it!).

Whilst these challenges may appear quite daunting for some, it is important to remember that change can also bring about opportunities for improvement. With the introduction of the new national system, it could be an appropriate time for schools to rethink their own SEN strategy. Here are a few questions schools may want to consider:

- Do we need to refocus on what is meant by 'special educational needs' within our school?
- How can we enhance the capacity and skills of our workforce to support pupils with SEN?
- How can we benefit from an increased choice over commissioned services for provision?
- Is it a priority for us to develop increasingly positive relationships with our parents and families and, if so, how?
- How can we increase the SENCO's influence over decision-making at a strategic level?
- What is the most effective way to evidence how changes in provision will result in better outcomes for pupils with SEN?

Whilst pondering the possible challenges and opportunities, SENCOs are also likely to be asking themselves: what are the implications for my role?

The regulations for SENCOs lay out the standard require-ments for the role as a starting point.[7] These state that the appropriate authority of a school must ensure that the des-ignated SENCO is someone who is a qualified teacher working at the school. The regulations also make it clear that any newly appointed SENCO who has not previously carried out the role for a period of more than 12 months must achieve the National Award in Special Educational Needs Coordination (NASENCO) within three years of appoint-ment.

The *Indicative Draft Code of Practice* outlines SENCOs' key responsibilities. It notes that the SENCO has an important role to play in determining the strategic development of SEN policy and provision in the school.

'The key responsibilities of the SENCO may include:

- ▪ Overseeing the day-to-day operation of the school's SEN policy

- ▪ Coordinating provision for children with SEN

- ▪ Liaising with, advising and contributing to the in-service training of fellow teachers and other staff

---

7   See DfE (2009), The Education (Special Educational Needs Co-ordinators) (England) (Amendment) Regulations 2009; to be replaced in September 2014 by DfE (2013), The Education (Special Educational Needs Co-ordinator) (England) Regulations 2014.

- Liaising with the relevant designated teacher where a looked-after pupil has SEN
- Advising on a graduated approach to providing additional SEN support
- Ensuring that the records of all children with SEN are kept up-to-date
- Liaising with parents of children with SEN
- Liaising with early years providers and secondary schools, educational psychologists, health, social care, and independent or voluntary bodies who may be providing SEN support and advice to a child and their family
- Being a key point of contact with external agencies, especially the LA [local authority] and LA support services
- Liaising with potential next providers of education to ensure a young person and their parents are informed about options and a smooth transition is planned
- Collaborating with curriculum coordinators so that the learning for all children is given equal priority
- Ensuring with the head teacher and school governors that the school meets its responsibilities under the Equality Act (2010) with regard to reasonable adjustments and access arrangements.

> The SENCO is responsible for ensuring that the school can track and record support plans and decisions for all the children with SEN in the school. SENCOs can be particularly effective when part of the leadership team.'[8]

The exact nature of the role is determined by the head teacher and governing body and so can differ from one school to another. However, it is useful to have an outline of general expectations that leaders can use to develop job descriptions or guide performance management discussions and that the SENCO can use to provide clarity over their day-to-day work.

In summary, the SENCO will be providing strategic direction and development, coordinating provision and tracking progress, along with leading and developing others. This will place you right at the heart of the school improvement process, meeting the needs of all pupils whilst providing a specialist focus for those with additional needs.

8   DfE (2013c), *Indicative Draft: The (0–25) Special Educational Needs Code of Practice*, p. 44.

Top tips

- Keep up to date with national changes by visiting the SEN section of the Department for Education (DfE) website: www.education.gov.uk/schools/pupilsupport/sen/

- Ensure you are familiar with the 2012 Ofsted framework and gather evidence against each of the four key judgements (see Chapter 7 for further guidance).

- Revisit your job description. Does it reflect the strategic elements of your role? If not, ask to meet with your line manager to discuss it as part of your performance management.

In brief

1. The main aim of the national changes in SEN is to improve the system so that it works better for young people with SEN and their families, resulting in enhanced outcomes.

2. The September 2012 Ofsted framework places a significant emphasis on provision and progress for pupils with SEN.

3. The SEN Code of Practice provides practical advice on carrying out statutory duties to identify, assess and

make provision for children and young people with SEN.

4. The SENCO should be central to the school improvement process, providing strategic direction and development, coordinating provision, tracking progress and leading or developing others.

5. Although the changes bring a number of challenges, they also bring opportunities to make improvements at an organisational level.

Chapter 2

Leading the way: providing strategic direction and development

'A SENCO's power of persuasion and influence to inspire others towards achieving common goals and shared values relating to SEN, is driven by their vision for SEN and their passion to do the very best for pupils with special educational needs within a school.'[1]

The move from a more traditional, operational middle-manager role to that of a strategic senior leadership role has, for some SENCOs, led to a significant change in their working practice. Strategic leadership involves developing vision and direction for growth and improvement in relation to SEN as part of a whole-school approach. It is only really possible to effect change through providing leadership at a strategic level. There are no requirements for SENCOs to be part of the senior leadership team (SLT). However, in most schools

---

1   R. Cheminais (2010), *Rita Cheminais' Handbook for New SENCOs*. London: Sage Publications, p. 24.

this would be recommended as it is easier to provide effective strategic leadership if you are part of the SLT or, at least, where the head teacher and governors understand the significance of the role and ensure you are empowered to fulfil it effectively.

The key aspects of strategic planning for a SENCO include:

- Establishing the school's long-term direction for SEN.
- Leading the development of an inclusive culture within the school.
- Effectively managing SEN resources (including TAs).
- Empowering stakeholders to be fully engaged in the SEN process.
- Developing a collaborative, multi-professional approach to meeting needs.
- Monitoring the effectiveness of SEN provision and its impact on progress.

The initial step in your strategic planning will be to develop a clear vision of SEN. Ask yourself: what will our ideal provision look like in five or ten years time? How will this be achieved? How will outcomes have improved as a result?

Your overall vision will then be translated into policy, outlining key information on identification, assessment, provision and expected outcomes. The current regulations[2] on what

---

2   DfES (2001), Education (Special Educational Needs) (England) (Consolidation) Regulations. SI 2001/ 3455. Available at http://www. legislation.gov.uk/uksi/2001/3455/contents/made (accessed 1 July 2013).

schools are required to include within their SEN policy will be updated in 2014. You will need to report to the head teacher and governing body on the effectiveness of the policy (see Chapter 6 for a checklist on reporting to the governing body). Although you should be regularly checking that practice matches policy, it is recommended that you complete a full review of your SEN policy every three years.

Top tips

- There is an expectation that you will involve parents in developing your SEN policy, so set up a parents' forum or similar group where contributions can be made.
- Publish your SEN policy on your school website or in leaflet form to give easy access to parents and other stakeholders.

Your policy will determine the direction of the school's SEN strategy. This, in turn, will inform your SEN development or action plan. This should highlight:

- Overall success criteria.
- Aims/areas for development.
- Actions to be taken.
- Who will take the lead/who else will be involved.
- Timescales (including start dates and end dates).
- Resources required (including costs, staffing and time).

- Plans for monitoring the actions (who, when and how).
- An evaluation against each aim/area for development/ success criteria.

The action plan should be an integral part of the whole-school improvement plan, and links between the two should be made clear. To the right is an example of a SEN action plan template.

An important step in the strategic process is to ensure *everyone* in your school understands the vision and shows a commitment to achieving it. This is often the most challenging part!

Leading the development of an inclusive culture

All teachers are teachers of pupils with SEN.

This should be the mantra of every fully inclusive school. As SENCO you need to be emphasising that raising achievement for pupils with SEN is a collective responsibility, and then challenging any complacency towards this objective. One SENCO in a secondary school had the above mantra written as a headline on every piece of correspondence she sent out to staff! In schools that are successful in promoting the achievement of pupils with SEN there is a strong sense of purpose and shared values and this promotes an inclusive

SEN action plan template

Date of plan: Lead person:

Whole-school priority/link to school improvement plan:

Success criteria:

Aim/area for develop-ment	Actions to be taken	Persons involved	Timescale	Resources (cost in £ and time)	Monitoring (who, when, how)	Evaluation comment
				Total cost:		

culture. Such schools develop effective ways of promoting these shared values – for example, appointing staff who identify with the values and taking opportunities to articulate the values during discussions with pupils, staff, parents and governors.

You may occasionally come across teachers who feel that there is a conflict between the drive to develop an inclusive culture and the pressure to meet the standards agenda. They may ask: how is it possible to raise overall standards when we are being expected to manage pupils with increasingly complex needs? So, how do you persuade staff that there isn't a conflict and that they are, in fact, both part of the same agenda – increasing achievement?

Case study

One SENCO from a secondary school in South East England recalls one of the challenges she faced when starting in her new job:

Many of the teachers still had the view that the SENCO was responsible for pupils with SEN and that the SEN department was a place to send pupils who 'weren't coping in class'. This was partly because some staff lacked confidence in meeting the needs of these students. I began to address the issue in a staff meeting by asking the question: 'If we are successfully including students with SEN in our lessons, is the

> *quality of our teaching different – is there something unique about inclusive practice or not?'*
>
> *After much discussion, staff came to the conclusion that many strategies that work for pupils with SEN will work for all pupils. This was a good starting point as teachers now felt this was manageable within their own teaching. We then went on to discuss the purpose of schools for all pupils and the importance of having high expectations for all as part of high quality teaching. I gave some examples of SEN students who were achieving well where high expectations were in place.*
>
> *Changing attitudes is not easy and there is still a way to go, but we have certainly made a positive start to the change process. All of SLT, including myself, make sure we reiterate some of these key messages whenever we can as part of our increasingly inclusive whole-school ethos.*

As SENCO you will need to be modelling the message that setting high expectations for all pupils, including those with SEN, is one of the most important things that teachers can do to ensure good progress in learning. Enhancing expectations will lead to improved outcomes for all pupils, and that is what makes a school really inclusive. Chapter 4 provides further detail on setting expectations for pupils with SEN.

Turning policy into practice: identification and assessment of needs

The *Support and Aspiration* Green Paper highlights the importance of early and effective identification of pupils' needs in order that support can be put in place as soon as possible. But how do you and your staff decide when a pupil has special educational needs? In their 2010 report, *A Statement Is Not Enough*, Ofsted noted that many children who have been identified as having special educational needs are, in fact, underachieving for other reasons.[3]

If a pupil is underachieving, it means they are not attaining at the level at which they are capable, and therefore are not reaching their full potential. There are many reasons why this happens; it *may be* because they have a learning difficulty. Whilst many pupils with SEN do achieve well and are able to reach their potential, others do not. Alternatively, underachievement may be the result of something that has recently happened to the pupil which has caused relatively short-term stress (e.g. bereavement). However, it may simply be because the teaching the pupil is receiving is not meeting their needs effectively.

---

3   Ofsted (2010), *A Statement Is Not Enough: Ofsted Review of Special Educational Needs and Disability*. Available at: http://www.ofsted.gov.uk/news/statement-not-enough-ofsted-review-of-special-educational-needs-and-disability-0 (accessed 17 June 2013).

So how do you determine the differences between underachievement and SEN? Here are some questions you might want to consider as a whole school:

▧ What percentage of pupils are identified with SEN? How does this compare with the national average of approximately 20 per cent? Does there appear to be over-identification?

▧ When a pupil is identified as underachieving, is there a process to explore the quality of teaching the pupil is receiving before considering if they have SEN?

▧ What additional qualitative and quantitative evidence do you use to clarify reasons for underachievement?

Top tip

▧ It is important to have clear and robust criteria about what constitutes SEN in your school, and that this information is shared and understood by all teachers.

Identifying a pupil's needs will involve using a range of data in order to establish a baseline. This will include analysis of the following examples of evidence:

▧ Attainment and progress data, including National Curriculum levels or sub-levels, GCSE predicted grades, average points scores (APS) for reading, writing and/or English and mathematics.

- Scores from standardised reading, spelling or mathematics tests.
- Other diagnostic assessment scores, such as non-verbal reasoning and Cognitive Abilities Tests (CATs).
- Year 1 phonics screening check outcomes.
- Analysis of the pupil's work.
- Observations of the pupil (in class and in less structured situations).
- Feedback from discussions with parents, pupils and staff.
- Attendance and behaviour data.
- Information from external agencies.
- Evidence of the impact of provision already tried (e.g. inclusive day-to-day teaching).

Analysing this information will help to establish the pupil's strengths and identify possible reasons for underachievement. For the majority of pupils, their needs can (and should) be met through the normal whole-school processes for assessing, planning, teaching, target setting, tracking and monitoring progress. However, where analysis shows that a pupil's needs require them to access provision that is *significantly different and more specialised* than the majority of their peers, then that is the point at which the SEN framework comes into play.

A graduated response

Where a pupil has been identified as requiring school-based SEN support, the school should ensure the following are in place:

1. A review of the quality of the day-to-day teaching the pupil is receiving and any changes required.

2. Opportunities for pupils and parents to be fully engaged in the process and agreement reached on how needs will be met.

3. A plan that focuses on what outcomes are expected and the support that the school, parents and any relevant agencies will provide (it doesn't matter what this plan is called – as long as it works!).

4. Effective communication with, and support for, any staff involved in implementing the plan.

5. Where relevant, external services and providers working in partnership with schools to meet the needs of the pupil.

6. Regular reviews of progress (e.g. at least once a term).

The reviews of progress should consider:

▓ Any changes required to provision, including increased or reduced intensity and frequency of support.
▓ The need for increased or decreased expertise.

▩ Where sufficient progress has been made, the continued requirement of additional support.

▩ Where progress has not been made, the need for further assessment.

In a minority of cases, where pupils have received ongoing additional support over a period of time, yet continue to make no or very limited progress, consideration should be given to requesting an assessment for an EHC plan. The SEN Code of Practice will provide further details on the process of requesting, drawing up, implementing, monitoring and reviewing an EHC plan.

The Equality Act 2010

The Equality Act 2010[4] replaced most of the duties in the Disability Discrimination Act 1995.[5] It states that schools cannot unlawfully discriminate against pupils because of their disability (or other 'protected characteristics' including race, religion and sexual orientation). The Equality Act states that a person has a disability if they have: 'a physical or mental impairment and the impairment has a substantial and long-term adverse effect on their ability to carry out normal day-to-day activities'.

This definition includes learning difficulties, language and communication impairments, mental health conditions and

4   Great Britain (2010), Equality Act 2010. Available at: http://www.legislation.gov.uk/ukpga/2010/15/contents (accessed 17 June 2013).

5   Great Britain (1995), Disability Discrimination Act 1995. Available at: http://www.legislation.gov.uk/ukpga/1995/50/contents (accessed 17 June 2013).

medical conditions. Discrimination includes treating a disabled pupil less favourably because they are disabled or
putting disabled pupils at a substantial disadvantage compared with another child who is not disabled. Every school,
therefore, has a duty to ensure discrimination does not occur.

Top tip

▪ Remember, not all pupils that fall under the
definition of having a disability will have special
educational needs. However, part of your role as
SENCO is to ensure that teachers are meeting the
needs of disabled pupils.

The Equality Act outlines the duties of schools to make 'reasonable adjustments' for pupils with SEN and disabilities.
This is known as the reasonable adjustments duty and
includes a duty for the school to provide auxiliary aids and
services for disabled pupils. When a school does something
that might put a disabled child at a substantial disadvantage,
compared with other children who are not disabled, the
school must take reasonable steps to avoid that disadvantage
under the duty. The SENCO must ensure that all staff are
familiar with the reasonable adjustments duty and what it
means for them in their classroom.

For many teachers, the good news is that they will already
be implementing reasonable adjustments every day – they
just might not realise it. A reasonable adjustment can be

something as simple as teachers being aware of the level of language they use or introducing buddy schemes to support access. Other examples include:

- Changing the classroom layout to provide better access for pupils with limited mobility.
- Displaying signs in a range of media (e.g. Braille, symbols).
- Providing a distraction-free learning area for pupils with autistic spectrum disorder (ASD).
- Ensuring the classroom has appropriate acoustics to support pupils with hearing impairments.
- Providing extra time for physically disabled pupils to use equipment in practical tasks.
- Pre-tutoring to improve access to lessons for pupils with learning difficulties.
- Providing access to technology for children with disabilities.
- Providing alternatives to written recording for pupils who find writing challenging.
- Making educational visits accessible to pupils with disabilities.

It might be helpful for the SENCO to provide staff training on the Equality Act – for example, by making available example scenarios to discuss what reasonable adjustments could be made. Of course, sometimes the issue may be more complex and it might be the attitudes and beliefs of staff that need adjusting – this can be difficult. Discrimination can occur unintentionally, so challenging staff on their beliefs may be the first step you take towards making a reasonable adjustment. Promoting fully inclusive practice is the next step.

In addition to their responsibilities to individual pupils, schools have more general duties under the Equality Act, covering disabled staff, parents and any other users of the school. These duties include the need to plan to make their school more accessible to disabled pupils and improve the equality of opportunity for disabled people. As part of the general duties, schools are required to produce accessibility plans every three years which will highlight their proposed strategies for:

- Increasing disabled pupils' access to the curriculum.
- Improving the physical environment so disabled pupils are not placed at a disadvantage.
- Improving the delivery of information to disabled people.

For more information on accessibility planning and the implications of equality law on schools, see the guidance for schools produced by the Equality and Human Rights Commission (EHRC).[6]

---

6   EHRC (2010), *Education Providers: Schools Guidance*. Available at: http://www. equalityhumanrights.com/advice-and-guidance/education-providers-schools-guidance/ (accessed 17 June 2013).

Top tips

- Knowing and understanding what your statutory duties are to your pupils with SEN is crucial, not only because you have a legal and moral obligation to do so, but also in order to avoid tribunal cases. Become familiar with your statutory duties and have a full understanding of the requirements of the Equality Act.

- The strategic role may be quite daunting, but remember you don't necessarily have to do it all yourself. Consider who else in your school/ department/team has the potential capacity to support you, and distribute some of your jobs to them.

- Sometimes you will need to make strategic decisions that might be unpopular. However difficult this might be, keep in mind that your job is to ensure the best for the pupils.

In brief

1. Strategic leadership involves developing vision and direction for growth and improvement in relation to SEN as part of a whole-school approach.

2. Everyone in your school needs to understand the vision for SEN and show a commitment to achieving it. There

should be a collective responsibility towards meeting the needs of pupils with SEN – every teacher is a teacher of SEN.

3. Early and effective identification of pupils' needs is essential in order that support can be put in place as soon as possible.

4. Where a pupil's needs require them to access provision which is significantly different and more specialised than the majority of their peers, they will need school-based SEN support.

5. The Equality Act requires schools to make 'reasonable adjustments' for pupils with SEN and disabilities. All teachers should be considering how they are implementing reasonable adjustments in their classrooms.

Chapter 3

High quality SEN provision – all day, every day

High quality, inclusive teaching is about meeting the needs of *all* pupils and having high expectations for *all* pupils, including those with SEN.

The 'job advert' at the start of the introduction to this book outlines some of the essential skills and qualities needed to be a great SENCO: efficient, organised, enthusiastic, flexible, motivational. All of these are indeed important but, above all, a SENCO has to be an *excellent practitioner*. Their key role involves ensuring that all staff are fulfilling their responsibilities towards meeting the needs of pupils with SEN – and what better way to do this than to be a good role model. Having a sound understanding of strategies for removing barriers to learning *and* being able to demonstrate these in practice in the classroom will go a long way in helping to raise the overall quality of teaching for pupils with SEN.

In their 2010 report into the teaching of pupils with SEN, Ofsted note that the key priority for all children must be 'good teaching and learning'.[1] This may sound like an obvious statement, but too often some of the most vulnerable pupils in our schools are not getting the highest quality teaching and learning. The starting point for ensuring this happens, as mentioned in Chapter 2, is that all teachers recognise that they are teachers of pupils with SEN. Indeed, the 2012 *Teachers' Standards* place a significant emphasis on supporting pupils with SEN. Standard 5 requires the adaptation of teaching to respond to the strengths and needs of all pupils. For example, teachers must:

'have a clear understanding of the needs of all pupils, including those with special educational needs; those of high ability; those with English as an additional language; those with disabilities; and be able to use and evaluate distinctive teaching approaches to engage and support them.'[2]

The role of the SENCO in supporting high quality, inclusive teaching

The fundamental principle is that high quality, inclusive teaching ensures that planning and implementation meets

---

1   Ofsted, *A Statement Is Not Enough.*
2   DfE, *Teachers' Standards*, p. 8.

the needs of *all* pupils, and builds in high expectations for *all* pupils, including those with SEN. This is a basic entitlement for all children and young people and should be underpinned by effective whole-school teaching and learning policies and frameworks. It is about the day-to-day interactions that take place in the classroom and the different pedagogical approaches teachers use to engage and motivate learners. It is about the way assessment and feedback is used to identify gaps and help pupils to move on in their learning. It is about providing both support and challenge in order to enable pupils to achieve more.

Top tip

▢ Make sure you prioritise the support for improving high quality, inclusive teaching – without this in place pupils will not make good progress, no matter how much 'different' or 'additional' support is given.

So, how can the SENCO help staff to understand what this might look like in the classroom? The following table highlights some of the key characteristics of high quality, inclusive teaching that should be evident in all lessons. The list is not exhaustive but is meant to be used as a starting point for discussion. Try giving the table to your teachers and asking them to identify how many of the following characteristics they consistently practise.

Key characteristics of high quality, inclusive teaching and learning	Is this consistent practice in my classroom?
High expectations are made explicit for all pupils.	
The classroom environment and resources provided support pupil learning.	
Lessons are well planned with clear and focused learning objectives and success criteria.	
Reasonable adjustments and special educational provision are planned effectively.	
A range of effective teaching strategies and approaches to support individual needs are in place.	
The teacher and other adults model and explain effectively.	
The teacher and other adults use higher level questioning to support and challenge pupils.	
There are high levels of engagement and interaction for all pupils.	

Opportunities for learning through individual and group discussion are provided.						
Opportunities for pupils to be working independently and collaboratively are provided.						
Effective feedback is used to move pupils on in their learning.						
Encouragement and praise are used effectively to engage and motivate pupils.						
Pupils are able to confidently and accurately engage in self and peer assessment to identify next steps for learning.						
Additional adults are deployed effectively to support pupil progress.						
As a result of the above, *all* pupils: ■ Show high levels of engagement with their learning. ■ Take ownership and responsibility over their learning. ■ Enjoy their learning. ■ Become increasingly independent learners. ■ Make progress.						

In order to develop high quality, inclusive teaching, the SENCO can support staff in a number of ways, starting with Assessment for Learning (AfL). High quality teaching starts with teachers knowing their pupils well and understanding their needs, potential barriers, where they are in their learning and what their next steps are. SENCOs can help teachers to:

- Understand children's cognitive development so they can spot where development is not following the usual pattern.
- Identify the specific strengths and needs of an individual and how this could impact on their learning.
- Understand potential barriers to a pupil's learning.
- Identify any gaps or misconceptions in learning.
- Set appropriately challenging targets based on a pupil's age and prior attainment, and also take into consideration the nature of their SEN.
- Involve the pupils themselves in setting targets and understanding how they can make improvements in their learning.
- Use questioning to effectively challenge pupils' learning.
- Help pupils to understand the process of learning through improving metacognition – thinking about learning.

Take a look at Jackie Beere's *The Perfect Ofsted Lesson* for guidance and tips that you can share with staff to support them with AfL and developing independent learners.[3]

Other ways in which the SENCO can support high quality teaching include:

- Developing wider curriculum choice through providing flexible learning pathways and opportunities.
- Helping to differentiate curriculum planning.
- Developing an understanding of strategies for removing barriers to participation and learning (see below for examples).
- Utilising a range of learning approaches including whole-class, group and paired work.
- Using information and communication technology (ICT) effectively to enhance learning.
- Giving pupils ownership and responsibility over their learning.
- Effectively deploying additional adults to support pupil progress.
- Managing behaviour through the use of consistent and structured approaches.
- Analysing data to ensure that teaching and learning is effective.

---

3 J. Beere (2012), *The Perfect Ofsted Lesson*. Carmarthen: Crown House Publishing.

You might, for example, choose to run whole-school training, work with targeted groups of staff or support teachers on a one-to-one basis through mentoring or coaching. These methods are explained further in Chapter 5.

Removing barriers to access, participation and learning

Sometimes teachers will need planning strategies to support pupils with particular needs – for instance, those who have ASD or dyslexia. There is not scope within this book to provide examples for every area of need that teachers may come across. However, a good starting point may be to provide teachers with the following list of generic strategies, which should also form part of high quality, inclusive teaching.

In order to remove barriers to access, participation and learning I do the following:

▨ Ensure my classroom is accessible to all pupils (e.g. appropriate seating, lighting and acoustics, resources available (including ICT)).

▨ Provide clear and consistent classroom rules and routines and use rewards and sanctions appropriately.

▨ Consider the differentiated needs of pupils when planning learning objectives and activities.

- Pre-plan with my TA to ensure they understand the needs of pupils and that their support focuses on learning and progress.

- Ensure pupils are clear about the structure of the day and use visual timetables where appropriate.

- Provide support for key vocabulary (e.g. work lists, displays, pre-teaching).

- Support pupils who have difficulty remembering instructions (e.g. provide pictorial instructions, ask them to repeat instructions back).

- Break down learning and activities into small steps.

- Provide concrete resources for pupils to use (e.g. objects, counters, photographs).

- Consider my use of language to support pupils with communication difficulties.

- Provide scaffolding to support learning (e.g. writing frames, graphic organisers).

- Use a variety of pupil groupings (e.g. paired work, mixed ability).

- Provide alternative ways of recording written information (e.g. ICT, Dictaphones, scribes).

- Link learning to pupils' own experiences and provide opportunities for reinforcing and transferring learning to other contexts.

For further guidance for staff, take a look at Nasen's training tool, A Whole School Approach to Improving Access, Participation and Achievement.[4] It includes useful tips for supporting pupils with moderate learning difficulties (MLD), behavioural, emotional and social difficulties (BESD), speech, language and communication needs (SLCN), autism and dyslexia. The web version of the Inclusion Development Programme (IDP)[5] also provides materials and resources that can be used to promote high quality, inclusive teaching – or Wave 1 provision, as it is also known.

The Waves of Provision model[6]

The Waves of Provision model provides a useful way of planning provision at all levels across a school in an inclusive way, where it is acknowledged that high quality, inclusive teaching is an entitlement for all but that some pupils will need something additional. In the waves model, high quality, inclusive teaching is referred to as *Wave 1 provision*.

---

4   Nasen (2012), A Whole School Approach to Improving Access, Participation and Achievement. Available at: http://www.nasentraining.org.uk/resources/ (accessed 17 June 2013).

5   DfE (2013), *Inclusion Development Programme* (updated web version). Available at http://www.idponline.org.uk/ (accessed 17 June 2013).

6   The Waves of Provision model was developed as part of the National Strategies in 2008 and has since been adapted by schools in a variety of ways.

Wave 2 provision is for those pupils who are working just below age-related expectations. It includes interventions, as outlined above, which are designed to increase rates of progress in order to enable pupils to catch up or get them back on track for meeting expectations.

Wave 3 provision is for those pupils who are working significantly below age-related expectations, many of whom will have identified learning difficulties. It aims to accelerate and maximise progress, minimising gaps in performance.

Intervention (Wave 2 and 3 provision)

Additional or different provision will often take the form of a well-structured, time-limited programme delivered to a small group of pupils or on a one-to-one basis. It can be built into mainstream lessons (e.g. as part of guided work) or occur outside, and in addition to, whole-class lessons. There is a wide range of interventions available, particularly for literacy, and it is important to consider the evidence into what works well when making decisions about which intervention to choose.

Conclusions from key research: literacy interventions[7]

■ Ordinary teaching ('no treatment') does not enable children with literacy difficulties to catch up.

■ Schemes for Key Stage 3 are few, but several work well for reading and *Grammar for Writing*[8] has great potential.

■ Schemes for children who struggle with spelling work best when highly structured.

■ Work on phonological skills for reading should be embedded within a broad approach.

■ Large-scale schemes, though expensive, can deliver good value for money.

■ Where reading partners are available and can be given appropriate training and support, partnership approaches can be very effective.

■ Good impact – sufficient to at least double the standard rate of progress – can be achieved, and it is reasonable to expect it.

---

7   See G. Brookes (2013), *What Works Well for Children and Young People with Literacy Difficulties? The Effectiveness of Intervention Schemes*, 4th edn. Bracknell: Dyslexia-SpLD Trust. Available at: http://oneeducation.co.uk/download/file/What_works_for_children_fourth_ed.pdf (accessed 17 June 2013), p. 18.

8   DfEE (2000), *The National Literacy Strategy: Grammar for Writing*. DCSF: 0107-2000. Available at: http://webarchive.nationalarchives.gov.uk/20100612050234/nationalstrategies.standards.dcsf.gov.uk/node/153924 (accessed 17 June 2013).

In their research paper, *Literacy and Numeracy Catch-Up Strategies*, the Education Standards Research Team observed there was less evidence for the effectiveness of numeracy schemes than literacy interventions.[9] However, they did note that much of the research on both literacy and numeracy interventions points to a number of generic strategies that appear to be particularly effective. These include:

- Early intervention.
- Coaching staff in specific strategies.
- Tailoring teaching to needs.
- One-to-one tuition.
- Peer support.
- Developing home–school relationships.
- Close monitoring of pupils' progress.
- Meta-cognitive approaches.

As SENCO, you will need to demonstrate that there is a good range of intervention strategies being employed and ensure all staff understand *what* is involved (particularly the learning focus). When delivered outside the classroom, an intervention should clearly link with the rest of the curriculum and be planned with the class teacher, who should also be given feedback so that learning can be reinforced. Any intervention

---

9   Education Standards Research Team (2012), *Literacy and Numeracy Catch-Up Strategies*. London: DfE. Available at: http://media.education.gov.uk/assets/ files/pdf/l/literacy%20and%20numeracy%20catch%20up%20strategies%20 in%20secondary%20schools%2027%20nov%202012.pdf (accessed 17 June 2013), pp. 2–3.

should also be carefully monitored to evaluate the impact on learning.

Top tips

- Don't try to implement too many interventions – focus on a few that you know work well. Quality not quantity is the key!

- Take a look at Jean Gross' *Beating Bureaucracy in Special Educational Needs*[10] for further examples of primary and secondary interventions available for literacy, mathematics and social and emotional learning.

Provision mapping

With a wide range of provision in place across the three waves, it is important that coordination is organised and strategic. A useful way to manage provision effectively is by provision mapping. This is an ongoing, self-evaluative process aimed at identifying and overcoming barriers to learning, and ensuring every teacher is responsible for the progress of every pupil. It involves identifying specific, targeted support for individuals and groups of pupils but it should also function as part of a more holistic process:

---

10 J. Gross (2013), *Beating Bureaucracy in Special Educational Needs*. London: Routledge/Nasen.

> 'Provision mapping takes into account the full scope of provision, including high quality whole class teaching, guided and group work and individual interventions in order to identify and overcome potential barriers to learning and meet the needs of all pupils within and beyond the school setting.'[11]

The process begins with evaluation of the effectiveness of that all-important high quality, inclusive teaching. This process is central to whole-school improvement and there should be a global expectation that *all* staff are striving to improve outcomes for *all* pupils.

A practical approach to provision mapping

There are many benefits to provision mapping. It enables schools to:

- Plan strategically to meet pupils' identified needs.
- Provide an overview of provision and demonstrate how support is deployed.
- Draw attention to whole-school teaching and learning as well as individual needs.
- Cost provision effectively and show value for money.

---

11 DfE (2011), Provision Mapping. Available at: http://www.education.gov.uk/schools/pupilsupport/inclusionandlearnersupport/onetoonetuition/a00199972/provision-mapping (accessed 17 June 2013).

■ Demonstrate accountability to parents, governors and Ofsted.

■ Reduce paperwork and make the SEN process more manageable.

■ Support the school to improve and evidence pupil progress.

Part of the provision mapping process includes the development of a provision map. As a tool this provides an at-a-glance overview of the responses planned to meet the needs of pupils with SEN or other vulnerable groups. The map itself is often focused on intervention or provision which is seen as additional to the normal curriculum offer.

Many schools find it useful to follow a six-step model such as the one below:

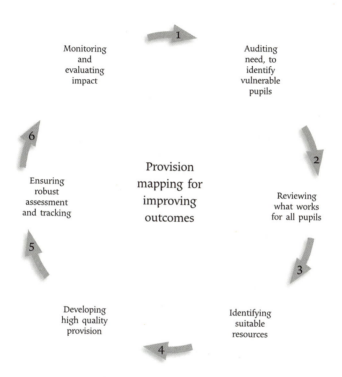

Step 1: Auditing need, to identify vulnerable pupils

▨ Identify target pupils: is your focus on SEN or are you going to include all vulnerable pupils (e.g. pupils in receipt of free school meals, looked after children, armed services children, pupils with English as an additional language (EAL))?

◾ Analyse information to make decisions about which pupils to prioritise (e.g. assessment and tracking data, pupil and parent views).

Step 2: Reviewing what works for all pupils

◾ Consider evaluations of your current provision: what works well and what doesn't work well?

◾ Investigate the findings from recent research on effective provision. In addition to Greg Brookes' research and work carried out by the Education Standards Research Team mentioned previously in this chapter,[12] you may find it useful to look at the Sutton Trust's *Teaching and Learning Toolkit*[13] and the Department for Children, Schools and Families' *The Deployment and Impact of Support Staff Project*.[14]

Step 3: Identifying suitable resources

◾ Identify your overall budget (see below for further details).

---

12 See nn. 24 and 27.
13 S. Higgins, M. Katsipataki, D. Kokotsaki, R. Coleman, L. E. Major and R. Coe (2013), *The Sutton Trust-Education Endowment Foundation Teaching and Learning Toolkit*. London: Education Endowment Foundation. Available at http://educationendowmentfoundation.org.uk/toolkit/about-the-toolkit/ (accessed 17 June 2013).
14 P. Blatchford, P. Bassett, P. Brown, C. Martin, A. Russell and R. Webster (2009), *The Deployment and Impact of Support Staff Project*. Research Brief: DCSF-RB148. London: DCSF. Available at http://www.ioe.ac.uk/diss_research_summary.pdf (accessed 17 June 2013).

■ Audit the availability, skills, knowledge and confidence of staff to deliver the provision and put in place any professional development required.

Step 4: Developing high quality provision

■ Confirm the provision you will be putting in place.

■ Decide upon the type of provision map you want to develop: do you want an overview map with provision and costings across the school or pupil-level maps showing provision for individual pupils (or both)? See the table below for an example of an overview map of provision for the three waves.[15]

■ Consider what other paperwork you might need to change, discard or develop to complement your provision map (e.g. pupil passports – see page 64 for an example).

Step 5: Ensuring robust assessment and tracking

■ Develop 'entry' and 'exit' criteria for interventions.

■ Identify processes for tracking pupils' progress, aligned to whole-school processes.

Step 6: Monitoring and evaluating impact

■ Establish systems for monitoring provision (e.g. data analysis, observations, gathering the views of pupils, parents and staff).

■ Use the outcomes of your monitoring to evaluate the overall effectiveness of provision on pupil progress.

---

15 For further examples, see my website (www.nataliepacker.co.uk) or that of SEN consultant Maria Landy (www.marialandy.co.uk/useful_info.aspx).

- Review the provision mapping process, identifying what worked well, what was cost effective and any areas for development.

This model will only work if provision mapping is an integral part of the whole-school improvement process, where all staff and other stakeholders, including governors and parents, understand the purpose and are involved in its development.

Example overview provision map

Area of need	Wave 1	Wave 2	Wave 3
Cognition and learning	Differentiated curriculum planning. In-class TA support or targeted teacher support. Visual timetables and other visual aids. Use of writing frames. Access to ICT. Team teaching/modelling. Access to whole-school homework clubs. Modified curriculum pathways. Basic skills course. Revision classes.	Literacy and numeracy catch-up interventions. Booster lessons. Exam booster classes. Targeted in-class support from TA. Reduced/increasingly individualised timetable. Guided reading within lessons. Integrated learning programme. Learning mentors.	Small group or one-to-one literacy/numeracy support. Reduced/increasingly individualised timetable. Exam concessions. Alternative accreditation/ vocational courses (e.g. ASDAN, Entry Level). Advice from educational psychologist/specialist teacher. SEN department homework club.

Area of need	Wave 1	Wave 2	Wave 3
Communication and interaction	As above (cognition and learning). Use of modified language. Use of symbols. Structured school and class routines. Environmental clues (e.g. location systems).	Targeted in-class support with focus on speech and language. Use of additional ICT.	Small group or one-to-one support for language. Social skills group. Speech and language support/advice. Makaton. Additional ICT – Writing with Symbols. Advice from educational psychologist/specialist teacher.
Emotional, behavioural and social	Whole-school behaviour policy, rules, reward and sanctions systems. Circle time. Lunchtime club. PSHE-focused work. Peer mediation.	Group circle time. Work-related learning. In-class support for supporting behaviour targets/access/safety. Additional tutor group support.	Small group or one-to-one support for social skills. Individual counselling or peer mentoring. Individual reward system. Social skills training or anger management. Reintegration programme.

	Social and Emotional Aspects of Learning (SEAL).		Advice from educational psychologist/specialist teacher. Pastoral support plan. Time out.
Sensory and physical	Flexible teaching arrangements. Soundfield system. Deaf-friendly initiative. Writing slopes and pencil grips. Brain Gym. Improved accessibility of building. Moving and handling training.	Additional keyboard skills training. Additional fine motor skills practice. In-class support for supporting access/safety.	Individual support for appropriate subjects (e.g. science, PE) in class or during lunchtime. Physiotherapy and occupational therapy programme. Access to PC with switch. Use of appropriate resources (e.g. radio aids). Advice from educational psychologist/specialist teacher. Signage.

Pupil passport

Name:	The things I enjoy or feel I am good at in school are …	My targets:
Date of birth:		
Date started school:	The things I don't like or don't feel confident doing in school are …	How I will help myself to reach my targets:
Photo:		
	I learn best when …	How others will help me to reach my targets:
My recent achievements:	My parents think that …	My targets review:
Signed:		Date:

Budget management and ensuring value for money

Do you know what your school's budget for SEN is or how it is spent? If the answer is no, you're certainly not alone. The SEN budget is not ring-fenced and, ultimately, the amount of money made available for SEN is at the discretion of the head teacher and governors. However, the management of the SEN budget is fundamental to the allocation of resources and support, so SENCOs need to be fully aware of the funds available.

All schools are provided with resources in their delegated budget that they can use to support pupils with additional needs, including those requiring school-based SEN support. The amount is determined by a local formula agreed with the Schools Forum. In addition, local authorities receive extra funding which can be used to provide further support for pupils with complex, high-level needs. However, the new funding arrangement makes it clear that schools should now be taking on greater responsibility for meeting the needs of all pupils with less complex needs through their delegated funding.

Developing costed provision maps will ensure that all interventions and additional support are accounted for financially. This will enable you to:

- Identify how much additional provision is costing.
- Identify how much you are spending on individuals or groups of pupils.

■ Clarify how you can meet the needs of all pupils within your allocated budget.

■ Make judgements about the effectiveness with which your school deploys resources to achieve value for money.

In short, detailed costings will support you in evaluating the impact of expenditure on pupil progress – something which Ofsted will want to know about when they visit.

Top tips

Simon Archer, SENCO and assistant head teacher at Bury Church of England High School, provides some guidance on provision mapping:

■ Remember there is no one-size-fits-all model to provision mapping and you will need to adapt processes to find what works for you.

■ The process needs to be manageable. Start simple and don't try to do everything at once. If you are a large school, perhaps focus on one particular year group.

■ Try carrying out an initial audit to identify what interventions are already in place and working well.

■ Consider how your provision map will link in with other documentation. If you're still using individual education plans (IEPs), could pupil provision maps, alongside pupil passports, be developed as an alternative?

- Make sure that provision mapping is seen as an integral part of whole-school provision and not as a bolt-on.

In brief

1. High quality, inclusive teaching is a basic entitlement for all. Without this in place, pupils will not make progress no matter how much additional support is provided.

2. The Waves of Provision model is useful for planning provision across a school in an inclusive way.

3. When making decisions about additional interventions, consider the evidence into what works well and evaluate the impact of your own interventions carefully.

4. Provision mapping is a useful way to coordinate provision effectively.

5. Having a clear overview of your budget and spend is essential to enable you to plan strategically.

Chapter 4

Tracking and monitoring to raise achievement

> The most important role of teaching is to raise pupils' achievement.

Undoubtedly, there isn't one SENCO out there who doesn't agree that all pupils can, and should, be making progress and that the job of the teacher is to remove any potential barriers to learning to ensure that progress happens. However, the issue of showing progress for some pupils who may make very small steps in their learning can often be a challenge. Teachers often ask: can all of my pupils with SEN *really* make two or three levels of progress across a key stage and, if we're raising expectations for all, can we *realistically* narrow the attainment gap between those with SEN and those without? These are not easy questions to answer, but the starting point is ensuring that everyone is clear about expectations around progress. Try discussing the following questions with your staff.

Does everyone in the school share an understanding of what good progress looks like for pupils with SEN?

As part of the school self-evaluation process, senior leaders will be closely analysing whole-school data in order to make judgements about attainment, progress and overall achievement. As SENCO, you will need to be able to extrapolate the data for SEN pupils in order to make your own judgements.

The 2012 Ofsted framework provides an increased focus on *progress*. Ofsted inspectors will take account of:

- The learning and progress across year groups of different groups of pupils, including disabled pupils, those who have SEN and those for whom the Pupil Premium provides support.

- Pupils' progress in the last three years, including that for looked after children, disabled pupils and those who have SEN.

- The proportions meeting and exceeding expected progress from different starting points compared with national figures.

The DfE and Ofsted define expected progress as:

- Two National Curriculum levels of progress between Key Stages 1 and 2.

- Three National Curriculum levels of progress between Key Stages 2 and 4.

The majority of schools work on an expectation of *at least* a three point score increase per year (converting sub-levels into point scores enables schools to track progress in smaller steps). This equates to satisfactory progress. Good progress would be demonstrated by more than a three point score increase per year.

There is clarity over nationally expected levels of attainment at the end of Key Stages 1, 2 and 4 which all SENCOs will be familiar with. But what about those pupils who are not working at age-related expectations – are they expected to make the same amount of progress? Ofsted's *School Inspection Handbook* provides further advice on evaluating the achievement and progress of pupils with SEN:

> 'For those groups of pupils whose cognitive ability is such that their attainment is unlikely ever to rise above "low", the judgement on achievement should be based on an evaluation of the pupils' learning and progress relative to their starting points at particular ages, and any assessment measures held by the school.'[1]

There is an acknowledgement that, for a small minority of pupils, they may never catch up with their peers. However, teachers should still be expecting these pupils to be making *at least good progress*. Using national expectations to set targets for all pupils ensures appropriate ambition.

---

1   Ofsted, *School Inspection Handbook*, p. 32.

Your school's RAISEonline data will support national benchmarking, providing information on end of key stage attainment and progress. For example, you will be able to extract information on how well pupils with SEN attained in relation to pupils nationally and in relation to pupils without SEN in the school. You will also be able to acquire information about value added and expected progress.

Another useful document for measuring and evaluating the achievement and progress of pupils with SEN is the DfE's *Progression 2010–11*.[2] This guidance brings together three key principles and three sets of national data to support schools in evaluating the progress of pupils with SEN. It enables schools to use national comparative data to support judgements about progress and expectations and to help set challenging and aspirational targets.

The three key principles within the guidance are as follows:

1. High expectations are key to securing progress.

2. Accurate assessment is essential to securing and measuring pupil progress.

3. Age and prior attainment are the starting points for developing expectations of pupil progress.

---

2   DfE (2010), *Progression 2010–11: Advice on Improving Data to Raise Attainment and Maximise the Progress of Learners with Special Educational Needs*. Available at: http://webarchive.nationalarchives.gov.uk/20110809101133/http://nsonline.org.uk/node/437685 (accessed 1 July 2013).

It is useful for SENCOs to share these principles with teachers as they underpin the use of data on attainment and progress for all pupils, including those with SEN. The ebook *Making and Measuring Progress for Pupils with SEND*[3] provides further information on using *Progression 2010–11* for data analysis.

Top tips

- Become familiar with RAISEonline. Talk to your line manager, assessment lead or data manager and ask them to take you through the latest version, pointing out which sections would be particularly useful for you to analyse.

- Plan opportunities for teachers to undertake joint standardisation and moderation activities, including a focus on P levels, to ensure assessment is accurate and consistent.

3   J. Martin (2012), *Making and Measuring Progress for Pupils with SEND: Strategies to Achieve and Demonstrate Progress*. London: Optimus Education. Available from http://www.optimus-education.com/shop/making-and-measuring-progress-pupils-send-strategies-achieve-and-demonstrate-progress-ebook/

Do we set challenging and aspirational targets for pupils with SEN?

In order for targets to be appropriately challenging, they should be based on at least expected progress, as described above. The target-setting process will begin with numerical targets which will identify the level (i.e. P level, National Curriculum level/sub-level, GCSE predicted grade) each pupil is aiming to reach by the end of the key stage – and the end of the year – within a particular subject. These targets will reflect the pupil's longer-term goals.

The tables in *Progression 2010–11* can be used for setting key stage targets. As one of the fundamental principles of the guidance states, age and prior attainment should be the starting points for developing expectations of progress. When setting targets for pupils with SEN, we also need to take into account the nature of the pupil's SEN, but we must not use a label as an excuse for poor performance. Targets in *Progression 2010–11* are given at upper, middle and lower quartiles. The upper quartile levels match national expectations and there is an expectation that targets will be set to at least these upper quartile levels. These targets may be used alongside other measures – for example, Fischer Family Trust (FFT) or Yellis. Targets should support pupils with SEN to make accelerated progress and close the gap between themselves and their peers.

Once numerical targets have been set, the next essential stage is to turn these into curricular targets so pupils (and teachers) know *what* they need to do in order to reach their goals. These targets might be linked to the whole-class English or mathematics curriculum or encompass wider aspects of learning such as communication. Targets are more likely to be achieved if they are linked closely to the work of the class as a whole and can be addressed through the teacher's normal differentiated planning. Where pupils are receiving additional intervention input, targets could be linked specifically to the aims and outcomes. These may go beyond academic targets and focus on other areas that are important for an individual, such as improving behaviour, developing social skills or becoming increasingly independent.

Once numerical and curricular targets have been set, and provision put in place for implementation, the next step is tracking progress towards the targets. Most schools now have very effective whole-school systems in place for monitoring pupil progress. Tracking SEN should be an integral part of the system, ensuring that teachers (and not just SENCOs) are responsible and accountable for the outcomes of all their pupils, including those with SEN. Many effective schools hold termly pupil progress meetings where the teacher and a senior leader have the opportunity to discuss in detail the progress of all pupils in a class, including those who have SEN or those who are underachieving, and consider the next steps for any pupils not on track to help them achieve their targets.

Case study

Andrew Crossley, assistant head teacher and inclusion coordinator at Highgate Primary Academy in Barnsley, shares the processes for tracking and target setting used in the school:

Initially, we plot the 'flight paths' of all pupils in the school to enable us to set clear and ambitious targets. Rigorous tracking of half-termly assessment data then ensures quick and timely identification of any pupils who are not on track and who may need further intervention or input from outside agencies. I also meet with individual teachers for one-to-one discussions about the progress of pupils with SEN and this helps to maintain a high profile of SEN across the school.

Targets for pupils with SEN are set and recorded in the form of IEPs. These are shared with all staff involved in support-ing the pupil to ensure that the steps to success are followed. The targets are linked directly to interventions, and this means that IEPs are used effectively as working documents to track and record progress specifically against the intended intervention outcomes.

At the end of each half term, children are again plotted against their own flight path and compared with national expectations. Targets are reassessed and new, aspirational ones are set, along with plans to help pupils achieve them. This rigorous and transparent process of assessment, tracking and target setting, alongside implementing focused provision,

> *has enabled us to successfully narrow the gaps between SEN*
> *and non-SEN pupils.*

Setting appropriate targets for individuals, which dovetail into whole-school target setting systems, can be challenging for some teachers, so this is one area in which the SENCO can provide support. Jean Gross' *Beating Bureaucracy in Special Education Needs* provides further guidance on setting, monitoring and achieving targets.

Is the attainment and progress of our pupils with SEN good enough?

Reviewing the attainment and progress of pupils with SEN should, again, be part of the whole-school system and take into account progress towards both numerical targets and curriculum targets. As part of high quality, inclusive teaching, class and subject teachers should be reviewing smaller step targets for individuals on a regular basis through an AfL approach. This may conclude with a formal termly pupil progress meeting and/or review with parents, the SENCO and other appropriate professionals. An evaluation of the effectiveness of the provision put in place to enable pupils to reach their targets will be a crucial part of this process. The review discussion should enable all involved to reach a judgement about the overall progress the child has made and what actions will need to follow to ensure progress is sustained or accelerated further.

Because the majority of schools have accurate and robust whole-school assessment, tracking and monitoring systems in place, the SENCO should have no shortage of attainment and progress-related data – but all that data is useless until you do something with it! The next step for you, therefore, will be to consider all of the evidence from the processes outlined above in order to reach a judgement about the overall attainment and progress of pupils with SEN across the school.

The prompt sheet below aims to support SENCOs with their initial data analysis.

Key questions for SEN data analysis

1. **How are pupils on the SEN record attaining in comparison with other groups across the school/ nationally?**

   - How are pupils with SEN attaining in relation to pupils with SEN nationally?

   - How are pupils with SEN attaining in relation to other groups across the school, including non-SEN?

   - How does this compare with previous years – is there a trend?

- How does attainment compare across different subject areas?

2. **What progress are SEN pupils making in comparison with other groups across the school/ nationally?**

   - What does the data tell us about value-added progress for pupils with SEN?

   - What does the data tell us about expected progress of pupils with SEN compared to other groups within the school/nationally?

   - How does this compare with previous years?

   - Is there a difference in expected progress made between English and maths/other subjects?

   - To what extent did individual pupils with SEN make expected progress?

3. **How do pupils working well below age-related expectations progress in comparison with similar pupils nationally?**

   - How are pupils working below national expectations achieving in relation to the national picture?

   - Are challenging targets being set for them?

   - Is there any variation in results between English and maths?

4. **How are individual SEN pupils currently attaining and progressing?**

   ▨ Are individual SEN pupils making at least expected or enhanced progress in core subjects?

   ▨ Are pupils on track to achieve their end-of-year/key stage targets?

   ▨ Is there any evidence of accelerated progress towards their targets and therefore the 'gap' narrowing?

   ▨ Where pupils have been involved in targeted intervention, have they made accelerated progress?

Considering these questions will provide quality evidence as part of your self-evaluation process (see Chapter 7 for further details). By following the analysis, you will be able to identify key areas for further development and record these on your SEN action plan.

Analysing other areas of progress

Analysing data against these prompt questions will help make judgements about attainment and progress, mainly within the core curriculum areas. As SENCO, you will also want to measure progress against other areas of pupils' learning, including attendance, behaviour, attitudes to learning, engagement, social skills, communication and interaction.

For measuring progress within the areas of behaviour, attitude or social skills a number of checklist type assessments are readily available that provide a baseline and which can then be used again at a later point to show progress (e.g. the Boxall Profile[4]). Asking for feedback directly from pupils, parents or staff can also provide qualitative evidence of progress.

Top tips

- Always include progress of pupils with SEN (and other vulnerable groups) as a key focus within pupil progress meetings. It is useful for the SENCO to attend these meetings where possible.

- As a way of evidencing both quantitative and qualitative progress for an individual pupil, try using a case study approach (see Chapter 7 for further details).

- Don't forget SENCOs have a responsibility to liaise with the assessment coordinator and examinations officer regarding access arrangements for the end of key stage external exams.

---

4 M. Bennathan and M. Boxall (2013), *The Boxall Profile Handbook (Revised)*. London: Nurture Group Network.

In brief

1. All teachers need to be clear about expectations of progress for pupils with SEN.

2. The SENCO will need a range of data to evidence the attainment, progress and achievement of pupils with SEN.

3. Age and prior attainment should be the starting point for developing expectations of progress.

4. *Progression 2010–11* enables schools to use national comparative data to support judgements about progress and expectations and to help set challenging and aspirational targets.

5. In addition to attainment and progress within English and mathematics, you will also need to measure progress against other areas of pupils' learning, including attendance, behaviour, attitudes, engagement, social skills, communication and interaction.

Chapter 5

Every teacher's responsibility: developing your colleagues

> 'For those children that face the greatest educational challenges, high quality teachers trained to support pupils with a wide range of SEN will be the most powerful way to drive up attainment.'[1]

Let us return to a key message running throughout this book: *every teacher is a teacher of special educational needs.* Easy to say; not so easy to achieve if you have any members of staff who still don't take full responsibility or have not had the opportunity to develop the appropriate skills to support pupils with SEN effectively. In Chapter 4, the importance of high quality, inclusive teaching was highlighted. In order for this to be in place, the SENCO needs to ensure there are good professional development opportunities for all staff.

---

1   DfE, *Support and Aspiration: A Consultation*, p. 58.

The role of the SENCO in continuing professional development

Initially, you will need to identify the continuing professional development (CPD) needs of all staff in relation to SEN. The SEN CPD audit table below can help you to do this. You will need to have knowledge of the range of CPD opportunities available for staff and support individuals and how to access them. This will include supporting trainee teachers, newly qualified teachers (NQTs) and staff who are new to the school in understanding the school's SEN policies and procedures, as well as providing general support to all on the use of effective strategies for meeting the needs of pupils with SEN. One way to do this is to provide whole-school training for staff – for example, on high quality, inclusive teaching.

Top tip

- There is a range of ready-made materials available on the internet to help you develop training sessions, so you don't have to start from scratch. Take a look at Nasen's A Whole School Approach to Improving Access, Participation and Achievement toolkit or the DfE's Inclusion Development Programme (IDP), both of which provide a range of resources to support staff with aspects of high quality, inclusive teaching and address specific areas of need.[2]

---

2 See p.50 footnotes 4 and 5.

SEN CPD audit

Question	Yes/No	Comments/Evidence
Are you familiar with whole-school aims/policy to meet the needs of pupils with SEN?		
Do you understand the systems and processes used for SEN?		
Do you feel confident in identifying pupils who may have SEN?		
Do you feel confident in your understanding of the range of pupil needs within your class?		
Are you confident in monitoring the progress of pupils with SEN?		
Are you confident of how well pupils with SEN should be achieving?		
Do you believe you provide reasonable adjustments to meet the needs of pupils with SEN?		
Do you use AfL effectively to increase the participation and engagement of pupils with SEN?		

Question	Yes/No	Comments/Evidence
Do you think that TAs are deployed effectively to ensure the support of pupils with SEN?		
Does the support you provide pupils with SEN improve their outcomes?		
What do you feel are your strengths in relation to supporting pupils with SEN?		
Is there anything that concerns you about supporting pupils with SEN?		
Are there areas of SEN which you would like further support with or additional CPD?		
Are there any other comments you would like to make about your SEN CPD needs?		

Name: Date:

Thank you for completing this audit.

Case study

A SENCO at a large secondary school in the East Midlands recently used the Nasen Whole School Approach to Improving Access, Participation and Achievement toolkit to provide INSET for NQTs. Having asked the NQTs to complete a SEN CPD, he identified that several of them were requesting further guidance on how to support students with dyslexia.

During a half-day training session, using some of the materials from the Nasen toolkit, the SENCO provided the group of NQTs with an overview of specific learning difficulties, tips for identifying students who may have dyslexia and strategies for supporting them in the classroom. He introduced the teachers to the 'dyslexia-friendly classroom' (see www.bdadyslexia.org.uk for further details) and, at the end, asked them to identify two changes they would immediately make in their classroom.

The SENCO followed up the training session by carrying out learning walks and having one-to-one discussions with each NQT. This helped to determine what difference the training had made to their practice and, most importantly, how the changes had helped dyslexic students to access the curriculum more effectively.

Whole-school or departmental training is often a time-efficient way to get a message across to a large number of staff. However, research has shown that one of the most effective ways of approaching professional development is by using collaborative approaches, where individual members of staff are supported by their peers in a more direct and often targeted way, such as joint planning, co-teaching or peer modelling.

Joint planning

Spending time with teachers during their planning sessions will provide a good opportunity for joint discussions around specific lessons. Colleagues can share ideas about:

- Identifying learning objectives/success criteria for lower ability pupils.
- Providing opportunities for pupils to work on their individual targets.
- Using strategies to enable the pupil to access the lesson.
- Developing differentiated resources (e.g. visual prompts, keywords).
- Effectively deploying TAs.

Co-teaching

Co-teaching not only enables two teachers to plan together but also to jointly deliver and evaluate a lesson. Although the idea of regular co-teaching is an unaffordable luxury in many schools, it may be possible for the SENCO to teach alongside another colleague for a short series of lessons. During a co-taught lesson there will need to be a clearly planned approach to the sharing of tasks and responsibilities, for example:

- Sharing whole-class teaching elements of the lesson.
- Carrying out guided group work with one or two different groups.
- Providing extra support and challenge for individual pupils with additional needs.
- Sharing opportunities for assessing pupils during the lesson.

Peer modelling

Where teachers may benefit from the opportunity to observe other colleagues' practice, the SENCO might carry out demonstration lessons. This provides an opportunity to focus on either generic or specific aspects of teaching practice, for example:

- Behaviour management techniques.
- Application of pedagogical approaches, such as the use of questioning to engage lower ability learners.
- Effective communication with TAs.

Similarly, this approach can also be useful for preparing TAs to run intervention groups, where the TA can observe a peer delivering a session before trying it themselves. The case study below highlights how one school adopted this approach and provided a range of opportunities for TAs to support each other in their professional development.

Case study[3]

At Overleigh St Mary's CE Primary School in Chester, SENCO Carol Hargreaves was keen to ensure that the school's deployment of TAs was focused on improving pupils' learning. Developing the skills of TAs through high quality training was therefore identified as a whole-school priority.

Following the introduction of new interventions, the TAs completed training to enable them to deliver the FFT Wave 3 Literacy Programme. The SENCO then provided opportunities for the TAs to engage in the following collaborative approaches:

- Peer–partner observations of FFT sessions with feedback.
- Peer mentoring by two previously trained and experienced TAs.
- A live teaching training session at a local professional learning centre, followed by detailed discussions about learning.

---

3 This case study by the author originally appeared in *Special Children Magazine* 210 (December 2012), entitled: 'Providing CPD through Collaborative In-House Approaches', pp. 19–20.

The feedback from the staff involved was very positive. The TAs reported that they felt more confident about delivering the intervention and had developed real insight into how to support pupils with literacy difficulties. Data showed positive outcomes and progress was made by all SEN pupils on the programme.

Alternatively, the SENCO may choose to undertake coaching or mentoring. The Centre for the Use of Research and Evidence in Education's *National Framework for Mentoring and Coaching* provides the following definitions of the two approaches:

Mentoring *is a structured, sustained process for supporting professional learners through significant career transitions.*

Specialist Coaching *is a structured, sustained process for enabling the development of a specific aspect of a professional learner's practice.*[4]

SENCOs are most likely to be involved in mentoring NQTs or other staff who have recently joined the school. Coaching may involve informal conversations to promote reflection on teaching practice or to support the development of more specific areas of SEN. Both approaches can be useful for moving on an individual's practice, but require the SENCO

---

4   CUREE (2005), *National Framework for Coaching and Mentoring*. London: DCFS. Available at: http://www.curee-paccts.com/resources/publications/ national-framework-mentoring-and-coaching (accessed 17 June 2013), p. 3.

to have time (often a luxury!) and a range of skills, such as active listening, questioning, reflection, sensitivity, and often patience, in order to be really effective.

So what difference has the CPD made?

Following opportunities for staff to engage in SEN CPD, it is important that the SENCO follows this up by evaluating the difference it has made to practice, and ultimately to the outcomes of pupils with SEN. It may be useful to ask staff the following questions:

- What aspects of your practice have changed as a result of the CPD?
- What difference has this made to your teaching?
- Has this had an impact on your confidence as a practitioner?
- How has this impacted on pupils with SEN? What difference has it made to their access, participation or achievement?
- Will this practice be applied in other contexts?
- Can this practice be shared with other staff?

Effectively deploying your TAs

In 2009, a major piece of educational research hit the media headlines and caused quite a stir amongst school leaders and staff. The Deployment and Impact of Support Staff (DISS) Project concluded that the more support pupils received from

TAs, the less progress they made.[5] Whilst some teachers say they would do (almost) anything to have more additional adult support in the class, the findings of the DISS project provided quite a wake-up call for many senior leaders. The report stated that it is not decisions made by the TAs themselves that cause the issues but rather decisions made by school leaders and teachers about how their support staff are used. Follow-up research published in 2013 reached similar conclusions.[6]

The future role of TAs is under great scrutiny and every school will have to carefully evidence that their support staff are providing value for money if they are to remain. When Ofsted are making a judgement on the quality of teaching, inspectors will look closely at how effectively support staff are being deployed. As a senior or middle leader, the SENCO has a responsibility for ensuring that the school is demonstrating good practice in deploying support staff so they *do* make a positive impact on pupil progress. So, what does good practice look like?

- TAs are given guidance and professional development on their roles, responsibilities and how to support pupil progress.
- Teachers are given professional development on how to make the most of TAs in their classroom.

---

5 P. Blatchford et al., *The Deployment and Impact of Support Staff Project*.
6 R. Webster and P. Blatchford (2013), *The Making a Statement Project: Final Report*. London: Institute of Education. Available at: http://www.schoolsupportstaff.net/mastreport.pdf (accessed 17 June 2013).

- Teachers and TAs have time to discuss planning, prepare for the lesson and feed back at the end of it.

- TAs understand the needs/targets of the pupils they are supporting and how to develop their learning skills.

- TAs are supported to use questioning and other AfL strategies to challenge pupils and move their learning on.

- TAs do not always support SEN/lower ability pupils – these pupils have equal access to support from the class teacher.

- TAs support pupils to become independent learners (no 'velcroed' TAs!).

- Senior leaders monitor the effectiveness of TAs (in class and when delivering interventions).

If you have line management responsibilities for support staff, your role will include being accountable for ensuring this good practice happens, in addition to developing their job descriptions, recruitment, induction, planning their day-to-day deployment, undertaking appraisals and providing professional development opportunities.

Case study

After becoming familiar with the outcomes of the DISS project, the head teacher and SENCO at The Weald School, in West Sussex, decided to review the way they deployed their TAs to ensure they were having an impact on pupil progress. SENCO Angie Burroughs notes that, previously, TAs had been used more generally to 'provide support in lessons for students with statements and at School Action Plus, as well as supporting teaching colleagues with differentiating materials'.

This has now changed through the development of 'learning mentors' posts. TAs who have become learning mentors are engaged more directly in supporting learning, either as part of the whole-class lesson or through focused intervention teaching in a small group.

Angie notes this is a much more effective way of deploying this group of talented individuals. The TAs report that they are working in a more purposeful way and their job is now clearly focused on supporting, monitoring and evidencing pupil progress.

Top tips

▪ Have a clear and transparent appraisal system in place for TAs to provide them with an opportunity to review their impact, set targets and discuss professional development needs.

▪ Ask pupils for their views on TA support (e.g. Which subjects do you prefer to have support in? What type of help is useful? Are there times when you prefer to work completely independently?) Their responses can help to inform your future deployment planning.

Don't forget yourself!

In this chapter we have looked at some examples of how you can support the CPD of others in your school. But there is one person we haven't mentioned – you! As part of your performance management, you and your line manager may identify and agree specific professional development opportunities, such as courses to attend or qualifications to take (including NASENCO where applicable). You may also want to consider some of the following options:

▪ Become a member of a national organisation, such as Nasen, which will provide access to a range of publications, local and national events and news. See www.nasen.org.uk for further details.

▓ Subscribe to a specialist journal or keep up to date by reading local or national SEN professional publications.

▓ Find out about distance learning opportunities – there are a number of online courses available aimed at SEN specialists.

▓ Set up a small group with other SENCO colleagues to meet regularly and exchange information and ideas.

▓ Join the Senco-forum, an email support network that links SENCOs across the country.[7]

▓ Visit SENCOs in other schools to observe their practice.

Top tip

▓ Develop a portfolio with examples of professional development you have invested time in as well as evidence of the impact this has had on your practice and the progress of your pupils.

In brief

1. The SENCO needs to ensure there are good professional development opportunities for all staff, starting with high quality, inclusive teaching.

---

7 The Senco-forum is hosted by the DfE. See http://lists.education.gov.uk/mailman/listinfo/senco-forum/

2. In addition to whole-school or departmental training, try a range of collaborative approaches, such as joint planning, co-teaching or peer modelling.

3. TAs require regular training and their impact will need to be carefully evaluated and recorded.

4. It is important to follow up staff SEN CPD by evaluating the difference it has made to practice, and ultimately to the outcomes of pupils with SEN.

5. The SENCO has a responsibility for ensuring the school is demonstrating good practice in deploying support staff so they make a positive impact on pupil progress and provide value for money.

6. In order to keep your skills and knowledge up to date, don't forget about your own CPD.

Chapter 6

Working in harmony: effective partnerships

> 'Every child who is disabled or identified as having a special educational need deserves our support, so that they, like every other child, can achieve their aspirations. We can only achieve that by working together.'[1]

How much of your time involves making telephone calls, arranging meetings with other professionals or communicating with parents? For most SENCOs, it is probably a significant proportion. Effective partnership working is essential to ensure that pupils with SEN are provided with the whole package of support they need. It is a key feature of the DfE's *Support and Aspiration*, which aims to make it easier for professionals and services to work together and to provide families with greater confidence in the services they use.

---

1 DfE, *Support and Aspiration: A Consultation*, p. 3.

Partnership working, however, isn't always straightforward and can present a range of challenges. Parents may have conflicting priorities to the school or may feel disengaged with the education system. Professionals from other services often have alternative ways of working to those in education – and different budgets. This is where SENCOs need to be demonstrating excellent interpersonal skills in order to facilitate the development of positive relationships.

As SENCO, do you have a clear understanding of the roles and responsibilities of all the following in relation to providing support for individual pupils?

Educational psychologist	Occupational therapist
Social worker	Counsellor
Educational welfare officer	Speech therapist
General practitioner	School nurse
Specialist teacher	Parents and families
Parent support advisers	Pupils
Physiotherapist	Police

And do they understand your role too?

It is important to be clear about lines of communication, management and accountability. You will need to be familiar with the professional language and terminology other practitioners use that differ to those in education and to understand the systems and protocols for information sharing. The use of technical jargon can be a barrier for some parents, so you will need to think carefully about the ways in which you engage with families to encourage positive relationships.

Top tip

■ Set *realistic* expectations about what can be achieved through partnership working with parents and other professionals within a reasonable timescale.

Partnerships with parents

The outcomes of the Lamb Inquiry[2] and the emphasis in *Support and Aspiration* on a more clearly defined role for parents in the decision-making process for SEN students, highlights the need for all schools to be prioritising effective partnership working with parents. The aim should be to enable parents to have a stronger voice in the SEN system and for professionals to treat parents as partners with expertise in their children's needs. Research has shown that enhanced parental involvement can have a significant impact on children's progress.

---

2   B. Lamb (2009), *Special Educational Needs and Parental Confidence: The Lamb Enquiry*. Nottingham: DCSF. Available at http://webarchive.nationalarchives. gov.uk/20130401151715/https://www.education.gov.uk/publications/ eOrderingDownload/01143-2009DOM-EN.pdf (accessed 17 June 2013).

The systems established within your school should help to empower parents to be involved in the following areas:

- Providing information and feedback to the school about their child and their needs.
- Setting and reviewing targets.
- Agreeing provision.
- Reviewing and reporting progress.
- Deciding appropriate ways of supporting the child at home.
- Involving the child in making decisions about provision and targets.

With the introduction of personal budgets, parents of pupils with an EHC plan will also be involved in deciding how their child's funding will be used. This makes it more important than ever that they understand their child's learning needs, the provision on offer in the local area and the effectiveness of different strategies. As SENCO, you have a responsibility to ensure parents have up-to-date information on the local offer so they can make informed decisions.

The need for the SENCO to have great interpersonal skills has already been highlighted. But what do parents think are the important qualities that make an effective SENCO? A group of parents of children with SEN in the West Midlands were recently involved in putting together a job specification for a new SENCO. The list below outlines the knowledge and qualities they prioritised:

- To know children with SEN on a personal level and understand the nature of their SEN well.
- To be willing to hold regular meetings with parents to discuss issues at home or school.
- To have good listening skills.
- To be sensitive to the concerns of parents.
- To be able to signpost parents to local services and networks.
- To be organised and punctual with paperwork.
- To be able to keep calm and professional in stressful situations.

The parents agreed that good communication was a top priority. They appealed for SENCOs to think carefully about how they make initial contact with parents as first impressions are very important. For example, when inviting parents into school, will the school phone, text or email them or send an invitation made by the child? The parents also appreciated flexibility around the timings of meetings in order to fit in with other commitments or practical considerations such as childcare or transport.

Case study

One parent of a child with SEN highlights the importance of good communication:

My son was born with complex difficulties and I spent a long time fretting about whether I would find a suitable primary school. After visiting several, I found a school where the SENCO was willing to really listen to what I had to say about my son and responded to my concerns in a realistic but positive way.

Once he started there, all the staff got to know my son very quickly and his class teacher was very willing to try out new things to support him. It's not always been easy but I know that if I have any worries at all, I can go to see my son's teacher or the SENCO, they will make time for me and together we can try and sort things out.

Many schools have well-established and effective systems for engaging the parents of all children, so SENCOs can build upon these procedures to carry out more targeted work with parents and families of children with SEN. However, some parents can find it a challenge to develop positive relationships with their child's school, perhaps because they had a negative experience of school themselves, have their own learning difficulties or are unsure of what to expect. Proactive schools seek to find solutions to engaging those parents who find it more difficult to build a relationship with them. Here are a few ideas that some of these schools have tried:

- Establish a Parent Partnership Coordinator role, enabling a member of staff to lead the work on partnership development.
- Set aside a space as a parents' room for parents to meet socially (it's often useful to start by providing parents with an informal and less threatening way in).
- Develop the role of parent mentors or buddies.
- Run parent and child workshops to demonstrate reading or spelling games that can be played at home.
- Establish a parent forum to provide mutual support and to contribute to SEN policy decision making.
- Develop podcasts to share learning with parents.
- Run parent and child after-school clubs (e.g. cooking, ICT).
- Hold a drop-in surgery at certain times during the week.
- Move meetings with parents into the community rather than being school based (e.g. local community centre, place of worship – or even the pub as successfully tried by one secondary school in Nottinghamshire!).
- Start relaxation workshops for parents (and possibly teachers too!).

Another successful approach tried by many schools is the introduction of 'structured conversations'. These are an integral part of the Achievement for All[3] initiative which aims to

---

3   See www.afa3as.org.uk/

improve outcomes for pupils with SEN and disabilities. The structured conversation is essentially a meeting between parents and a key teacher where quality time is made available for the teacher to listen to the parents' views and concerns. The teacher is trained in the skills needed to hold the conversation. Schools implementing structured conversations have seen significant improvements in their relationships with parents and this had led to a positive impact on the child's learning and overall attitude to school.

Top tips

- Do you know what parents' views are of the school's current SEN systems, provision and outcomes? If not, hand out a questionnaire or hold a focus group discussion (see the example questionnaire below).

- Consider how you provide information to parents. Check that it is concise, easy to understand and non-patronising. Translation into community languages may also be appropriate.

- Support parents to interpret reports from external agencies so they can obtain a full understanding of the implications for their child.

- Where you are making changes to SEN provision or systems for communicating, discuss these with parents and give them opportunities to input their views.

Example SEN questionnaire for parents

If you are happy to give your name, please write it here:

	Please tick (✓)		
	Yes	Partly	No
1. The school understands my child's needs			
2. The school tells me about my child's learning and progress			
3. Teachers give me support to help my child at home			
4. Teachers listen to my concerns			
5. I am pleased with the progress my child is making			
6. My child is happy at school			

				Excellent	Good	Satisfactory	Poor
7. I know the staff who support my child							
8. I am happy with the help my child receives							
9. The school and I work together to plan how my child's needs will be met							
10. I am involved in reviewing my child's needs							
Overall, I feel what the school does for my child is (please tick):							

Are there any other comments you would like to make?

Thank you for completing this questionnaire.

Chapter 6

Involving pupils

Children and young people with SEN have a unique understanding of their own needs and often have clear views about
the sort of help they would like. This means they are well
placed to be involved in making decisions, exercising choices
and expressing a preference about how their needs and goals
can be met. The expectation that schools will place not only
parents but also their child right at the heart of the processes
and decisions that will affect their lives is a central message
in the Children and Families Bill. In practice, this means:

- Encouraging pupils to talk about their strengths, needs
and ambitions.

- Asking pupils about what they feel they need to learn
and the type of help they find useful.

- Developing target-setting processes that pupils can take
ownership of and be responsible for working towards.

- Involving pupils in monitoring their progress and
evaluating their own performance.

- Seeking pupils' views as part of the statutory assessment
process.

- Engaging pupils in drawing up individual EHC plans.

- Involving pupils in all individual reviews and
reassessments.

- Taking pupils' views into consideration when planning
and reviewing the local offer (or the school offer).

How are schools involving pupils?

Many schools will have a range of effective approaches for supporting the participation of all pupils – for example, embedding AfL strategies or developing pupil forums. Here are a few additional ideas for ensuring pupils with SEN are fully involved:

- Self-advocacy training to support pupils with SEN to become more confident in expressing their views.
- Opportunities for pupils with SEN to be involved in drawing up policies or SEN information.
- Peer-mentoring schemes (e.g. for supporting transition for SEN pupils).
- Opportunities for pupils to lead their own reviews by taking responsibility for developing the agenda and leading the discussion.
- Alternative ways for pupils to record their views (e.g. video, blogging, email, drawings, mind maps).
- Person-centred planning (see below for details).

Person-centred planning (PCP) is an approach based upon a set of shared values which can be used when developing and reviewing support processes with a child or young person. PCP can be used to help the child think about what is important in their lives now and what will be important for their future. The planning process involves all the people who are significant in the child's life (their 'circle of support', such as family, teachers, support staff, friends, social workers, etc.).

The group meet on a regular basis to plan, review progress and identify next steps. The ultimate aim is that the child and their circle of support are able to identify for themselves what's working well, what's not working so well and how everyone can contribute to helping the child achieve their goals.

With PCP, responsibility is handed to the pupil. The meeting is theirs and they are encouraged to be involved in making decisions. For some pupils this can be quite challenging and they will need support and training to enable them to do this effectively. Central Lancashire's Person Centred Planning website offers further information and a number of useful tools that schools can use to support the PCP approach.[4]

PCP can also be useful for supporting the transfer process. Transition from one school to another – or even from one class to another – can be a particularly stressful time for pupils with SEN. As SENCO, you will need to liaise with any other staff who take a lead on transfer or SEN in the schools involved. Pupils with SEN may benefit from additional opportunities to discuss their concerns or have an extra visit day to help them prepare.

---

4   See www.csrpcp.net/default.aspx?page=16595/

Top tips

▓ Consider the use of pupil passports (see the example in Chapter 3) as a way of enabling pupils to communicate important information about themselves and to support them in taking ownership of their learning needs and progress.

▓ Ensure there is representation from pupils with SEN on pupil forums.

▓ Avoid tokenistic pupil voice. Check that pupils fully understand the reasons why they should be involved in making decisions. Thank them for their contributions and explain how their views will be valued.

The SENCO as commissioner of services

An increasingly important role for SENCOs is the commissioning of external services to provide additional capacity and support for SEN provision. This may be for an individual pupil assessment, specialist input such as therapy or to support staff CPD. SENCOs will need to be involved in researching service provider options under the local offer, exploring models of service delivery, brokering support from various sources and quality assuring the services commissioned. For many SENCOs, this aspect of their role may be new and pose quite a challenge.

Firstly, you will need to find out about the range of services available in your area. These may be provided by:

- The local authority.
- Community or voluntary organisations.
- Charities or trusts.
- Private organisations.
- Other local education providers, including teaching schools.

Many SENCOs are finding that access to certain services can be limited, particularly in the current climate of change. With an open-ended demand for services and, often, diminishing staffing levels, services such as educational psychology and speech and language are having to manage their time and resources even more efficiently than ever. Once again, effective communication, along with good organisational skills, is essential to help you manage the process.

Case study

Caroline Annetts, SENCO at Northowram Primary School in Halifax, explains how she promotes partnership working with external agencies:

I have found that one of the most challenging aspects of the SENCO role has been learning the correct protocol and pathways for referring to external agencies. As part of a referral,

I write a covering letter outlining our concerns and, crucially, what we have done to address the issue so far. I find external agencies are far more likely to engage promptly if they know we've been proactive in trying to meet the needs of the pupil and have accessed the more general resources they provide to all schools.

As I send a referral off, I make a note in my diary to chase it up in about three weeks time and check it has been received. This enables me to keep on top of referrals and ensure they don't get lost in the system. Once a professional from the agency has been involved with the pupil, I read their subsequent report and then meet with class teachers and parents to talk them through, ensuring the recommendations feed into upcoming targets and provision. As SENCO, I take responsibility for moving this forward. I also make the time to feed back to external agencies about the impact of their recommendations on pupil progress.

The outcome is a positive, productive and professional multi-agency partnership resulting in our pupils receiving specific, expert help within a relatively short time frame and consequently making accelerated progress.

Being proactive and establishing your own regular in-school partnership meetings can be useful. One example of this is the team around the child (TAC) approach. The TAC is a multidisciplinary group of practitioners established on a case-by-case basis to support a child and their family. This model of service delivery involves:

- A joined-up assessment.
- A lead professional to coordinate the work.
- The child/young person and their family at the centre of the process.
- Regular meetings involving the child/young person and their family and all professionals involved to discuss the support plan established to meet the needs of the child.

The TAC approach provides a structure for SENCOs and multi-agency practitioners to communicate in a meaningful way on a regular basis, often face to face. The approach is often used to support the Common Assessment Framework (CAF) process. CAF is a standardised approach used by multi-agency practitioners to assess children's needs and decide how these should be met. Further information can be found on the DfE website.[5]

Quality assuring any services you commission is essential – you need to check you are getting value for money! The most effective way to do this is by arranging discussions or carrying out surveys with parents, pupils, staff and service providers. Ultimately, you need to ensure that everyone is working towards the same goal: improving outcomes for the pupil(s). There should be a joint accountability process

---

5 See www.education.gov.uk/childrenandyoungpeople/strategy/integratedworking/
   a0068944/team-around-the-child-tac/

agreed between all parties for gathering, evaluating and act-
ing upon evidence of pupil attainment and progress.

Top tips

- Get in contact with your local teaching school and
  find out what SEN-related services they offer.
- Keep a record of meetings you have with parents or
  external agencies and make a note of any significant
  discussions, phone calls, emails or letters.
- Consider opportunities for inter-professional CPD –
  for example, joint training sessions for SENCOs from
  local schools and multi-agency partners.

Working with your SEN governor

Most governing bodies will appoint someone to take lead
responsibility for ensuring they fulfil their statutory responsibilities for pupils with SEN. One of the roles of the SEN
governor is to provide support for the SENCO and to challenge them to ensure they are providing the best for the
school and the pupils. For the SENCO, working closely with,
and getting the SEN governor on side, can be very handy.

The SEN governor will have a key role to play in monitoring
the provision for pupils with SEN and, alongside the SENCO,

will act as a champion for these pupils. This means they should:

- Be involved in the appointment of the SENCO and ensure the SENCO has the appropriate skills/experience.
- Be involved in SEN policy development and review.
- Keep up to date with local and national SEN legislation and developments.
- Have an understanding of the views of parents and pupils about provision.
- Monitor the school's SEN budget and spend to ensure value for money.
- Be kept informed of the progress and attainment of pupils with SEN.
- Contribute to the school's self-evaluation of SEN provision and outcomes.

Top tips

- Invite your governor to attend or contribute to SEN staff meetings or CPD sessions, particularly where you are providing important information (e.g. updates on changes to the SEN system).
- Arrange to meet with your SEN governor on a regular basis to keep them updated and involved. Make sure you go to the meeting well prepared (see the checklist overleaf).

Reporting to the governing body: checklist for SENCOs

Questions the governing body will ask	Evidence checklist for the SENCO
What is the profile of SEN in our school?	SEN profile (e.g. numbers of pupils with SEN, changes from previous years, significant groups).
What is the overall progress and attainment of pupils with SEN in our school?	Achievement and progress of pupils with SEN (e.g. end of key stage outcomes, percentage achieving national expectations, progress data). Percentage of attainment gap between SEN and non-SEN pupils in the school. Summary of attendance/exclusion and behaviour incident data for pupils with SEN.
How does the progress and attainment of pupils with SEN compare to national figures?	As above. Summary of RAISEonline SEN data.
Are SEN resources being used effectively?	SEN budget allocation. Changes in SEN staffing. Significant resources use, including external support.

Is the provision for pupils with SEN effective and does it provide value for money?	Summary of any changes in provision. Summary of evidence of effectiveness of provision, including interventions.
What are the views of parents regarding the effectiveness of provision?	Summary of feedback from parents. Number of parental complaints or appeals.
What has been the impact of any SEN professional development for staff/the SENCO?	Professional development log summary. Examples of impact evidence (e.g. observation summary, feedback from staff).
Is the school meeting its statutory duties, including those under the Equality Act 2010?	Summary of progress made towards the accessibility plan. Summary of progress made towards equality objectives.
Overall, how well is provision for pupils with SEN meeting needs and supporting improved outcomes?	Summary statement covering the quality of SEN provision and its impact (taken from self-evaluation). Summary of identified strengths and areas for development. SEN action plan and review summary.

In brief

1. Partnership working is a key feature of *Support and Aspiration*, with professionals working together more effectively to provide families with greater confidence in the services they use.

2. SENCOs need excellent interpersonal and organisational skills for partnership working.

3. There is an expectation that schools will place parents and pupils right at the heart of the processes and decisions that will affect their lives.

4. An increasingly important role for SENCOs is the commissioning of external services to provide additional capacity and support for SEN provision.

5. The SEN governor provides support for the SENCO and challenges them to ensure they are providing the best for the school and the pupils.

Chapter 7

Bringing it all together: self-evaluation and Ofsted

Imagine the scene: the head teacher calls all staff to an impromptu meeting to give you some news. You all know what it's about – you've been expecting 'the phone call' for a while. And here it is – Ofsted are on their way. They will be arriving the very next day. As mentioned in Chapter 1, the emphasis for inspection is very clearly targeted at those pupils who are vulnerable and who are underachieving or not making progress. So, for the SENCO, the stakes are high and your school is depending on you. The key to surviving your inspection? Be prepared.

Put simply, you need to be clear on:

- What you are doing and how you are doing it.
- Why you are doing it.
- What's working well and what's not working so well.
- How you plan to make improvements.

The main evidence for inspections will come through data analysis, lesson observations, scrutiny of work and discussions with pupils, parents and staff. The information gathered by inspectors during the visit will be triangulated with the evidence from the school's own evaluations. Making a judgement on the school's ability to self-evaluate is a major part of the inspection framework.

The overall responsibility for gathering the evidence of a school's effectiveness lies with the leadership of the school. However, as SENCO (whether or not you are part of the SLT) you will have a significant role to play in the self-evaluation process and in gathering evidence to show the effectiveness of SEN provision on progress. This is part of the whole-school improvement strategy and is especially important in evaluating how well the school helps the most vulnerable children make good and outstanding progress.

Monitoring and evaluating the impact of provision

Including SEN as part of the regular cycle of school improvement and self-evaluation will enable you to make strategic decisions about how to plan for improvements in provision. You will also be able to come to clear judgements about the impact of provision and develop effective support for colleagues. Effective monitoring and evaluation will be key to gathering the evidence and forming judgements.

In order to get a true picture of what is happening in your school you will need a range of quantitative and qualitative evidence. Mirroring the processes Ofsted will use to gather evidence during an inspection, here are some examples of tools you can use:

1. *Data analysis*

   Firstly, start by analysing your SEN record to identify where the vulnerable groups are and determine if there is possible over-representation of pupils within a group. Find out if there is any movement (e.g. the percentage of pupils no longer requiring school-based SEN support). Secondly, carry out data analysis for individuals and groups using national comparative data (e.g. RAISEonline or *Progression 2010–11*) and school-level tracking data. (See Chapter 4 for some key questions on SEN data analysis to support this process.)

2. *Lesson observations or learning walks*

   Observations or learning walks will provide you with first-hand, real-time evidence of the quality of teaching and learning. Your observations could focus on whole-class inclusive teaching strategies, support for lower ability pupils within a differentiated curriculum, effective use of TAs or the quality of small group interventions.

3. *Work scrutiny*

   Scrutiny of books, portfolios, pieces of writing or any other recorded examples of pupils' work can also provide evidence of the quality of teaching and learning. It can reveal whether the teaching leads to application of learning and can show progress over time, as well as providing information on the quality of written feedback provided by the teacher. You may choose to focus on work samples of SEN pupils or look across the ability range to make judgements on differentiation.

4. *Gathering views of stakeholders*

Providing opportunities for pupils, parents, staff, governors, external agencies and other stakeholders to express their views on SEN provision enables them to be part of the process and contribute to the development of provision. This can be done through informal discussions, interviews, questionnaires or surveys.

Top tips

- As part of your overall SEN action plan, include monitoring activities linked to the key priorities. Timetable the activities over the year to make the process manageable.

- Don't think you have to collect all the evidence yourself. All staff, including TAs, can contribute to gathering evidence of the impact of interventions.

- Where you have good relationships with parents, ask them to provide you with testimonies to show how pleased they are with the provision you are making for their child.

Chapter 7

Pupil case studies

There is a chance that inspectors will ask for examples of case studies for particular pupils in order to find out the 'story' behind their data. There is no knowing which pupils they will ask about – it may be a pupil who appears to have made little progress or it may be one who is also eligible for free school meals. If this happens, there will be little time to prepare. SENCOs often wonder, therefore, if they should compile case studies in advance. Perhaps, in an ideal world; so you may want to think about which pupil(s) the inspectors might choose based on the evidence they will have seen previously. However, in reality you can only prepare a few beforehand and these should form part of your normal self-evaluation process.

The trick is to ensure you have all the evidence to hand that you will need to put together a case study. This means that the existing systems and processes you have in place need to support the collation of evidence over the short, medium and long term. Within your case study you will want to include:

- Pupil details (e.g. year group, areas of need).
- Provision put in place (e.g. provision map, pupil passport, timetables).
- Summary of progress made over time, including teacher assessments, National Curriculum or P scale data, and other quantitative data such as reading age or spelling age.

- Impact of specific interventions (e.g. literacy or numeracy catch-up programmes).
- Summary of qualitative evidence (e.g. discussions with the pupil and parents).
- Evidence of involvement from external agencies (e.g. educational psychologist reports, health reports, social services reports).
- Any other documentation (e.g. meeting minutes, letters to parents).

There is no one preferred way to construct a case study and neither is there a particular format that Ofsted expect you to use. However, having all the information about a particular pupil in one place means you can use the case studies as a key part of your evidence in your meeting with the inspector during the visit, highlighting individual success stories and giving examples of how you have supported pupils to overcome barriers to learning.

Top tip

- If you have prepared case studies in advance of your inspection visit, make sure you hand them to the inspectors as soon as you can. If they are happy with what they see, they are less likely to ask for more!

Using your evidence to make judgements and prepare for Ofsted

As part of their self-evaluation process, schools will collect evidence to justify their effectiveness within the four key judgements of the Ofsted framework. Although no longer statutory, many schools still complete a self-evaluation form or similar document as a way of recording the outcomes of this process. It is useful for the SENCO to develop their own SEN self-evaluation document, which can contribute to the whole-school one. Recording outcomes from your monitoring and evaluation will enable you to make judgements about the overall quality of provision and progress made by pupils with SEN within the four key areas of the framework. The following lists provide examples of evidence that you will need to gather to make these judgements.

The achievement of pupils at the school

- An analysis of the data showing value-added progress for individual pupils according to their age and prior attainment.

- An analysis of any trends within the data over the last three years.

- An evaluation of this data to show how well pupils have progressed, using comparative data such as *Progression 2010–11.*

- Evidence of your identification processes, showing how you identify pupils who are vulnerable, those who have identified special educational needs and those who are underachieving.

- Examples of moderation of teacher assessment (including P levels) both from within the school and across different schools, where possible.

- Impact of interventions on pupil progress, particularly in literacy.

Top tip

- Know your data well and be able to tell the story behind it. Where pupils appear not to have made progress, make sure you can explain the reasons, describe what provision you have already put in place and be clear about the next steps for the pupil.

The quality of teaching

- Evidence that all staff understand and meet their responsibilities towards pupils with SEN.

- Outcomes of lesson observations, including small group interventions or learning walks, focusing on the quality of teaching and learning for pupils with SEN.

- Evidence that teachers are using assessment effectively to plan appropriate learning opportunities and set high expectations for pupils with SEN.

- An evaluation of how effectively support staff are used to improve pupil progress.

▓ Evidence of the effectiveness of professional development opportunities for ensuring teachers have the knowledge, skills and understanding to support and challenge pupils with SEN.

Top tip

▓ Ofsted will want to see all pupils making progress within observed lessons. Support teachers to provide opportunities for pupils with SEN to demonstrate the progress they have made in a short space of time.

Behaviour and safety

▓ Analysis of the representation of pupils with SEN in relation to attendance, punctuality, exclusions and bullying, and how the school is addressing any disproportionality.

▓ Information on the behaviour of pupils with SEN, how safe they feel in school and their attitudes towards learning.

▓ Careful tracking of the support for, and progress of, pupils with behavioural, social or emotional difficulties.

▓ Evidence of how the school addresses any punctuality issues caused by transport difficulties (Ofsted no longer accept this as an excuse for lateness).

Top tip

▦ Inspectors will spend time talking with pupils about their attitudes towards learning. Some pupils with SEN may need preparing for these conversations. Make sure you inform the inspectors of any pupils who may find this experience challenging.

Leadership and management

▦ Evidence that there is SEN representation on the leadership team and that governors are ensuring the SENCO has QTS (and has achieved the NASENCO, if appropriate).

▦ Evidence that the leadership team models high expectations for all, including those with SEN.

▦ Accurate information on the identification of pupils with SEN and the quality of teaching they receive.

▦ Evaluation of how well the curriculum meets the needs of pupils with SEN and provides for full access and participation.

▦ Evaluation of the progress made by individual pupils with SEN and other vulnerable pupils.

▦ Analysis of the views of parents about SEN provision and progress and any changes made in response.

▦ Evidence of a planned approach to SEN professional development for all staff.

■ Evidence that governors are aware of the quality of provision and progress of pupils with SEN and that they support and challenge leaders accordingly.

Top tip

■ Have an action plan in place that links to whole-school improvement planning. Include actions which recognise how you are intending to meet the changes to the SEN system. (See Chapter 2 for an example of an action plan template.)

Making an overall judgement on provision and progress

So now you have your evidence, how do you make an overall judgement? Aiming for the following aspects of outstanding provision and progress should be your ultimate goal:

■ All pupils with SEN make good or better progress in English and maths.

■ The gap between pupils with SEN and without SEN is narrowing.

■ Interventions for pupils with SEN are having a positive impact on pupil outcomes.

■ The quality of teaching and learning of pupils with SEN is consistently good or better.

■ Assessment is used effectively to target pupils' needs, develop appropriate provision and increase their rates of progress.

■ Pupils with SEN become independent and resilient learners.

■ The leadership of the school ensures that curriculum planning and access and support arrangements provide a high quality educational experience for pupils with SEN.

Where your evidence suggests that aspects of the provision and progress for your pupils is not yet outstanding, you can show how you will target these as part of your short-, medium- and long-term action planning.

Top tips

■ Take a look at www.nataliepacker.co.uk for examples of pro formas for supporting the monitoring and evaluation process.

■ Compile 'evidence folders' that you update on a regular basis and which provide a summary of the evidence, an evaluative judgement and an indication of next steps. Get into the habit of documenting everything you do. The checklist below provides a list of the documentation you may want to gather for your evidence file.

SEN evidence file checklist

- Summary of key 'headlines' around outcomes and an overall judgement on the school's evaluation of provision and progress
- Key strategic documents, e.g.
  - SEN action plan (with links to school development plan)
  - SEN policy
  - Reference to other relevant policies and plans (e.g. behaviour policy, equality plan, accessibility plan)
- Staffing information (SENCO and SEN team), e.g.
  - Names and roles
  - Example job descriptions
  - Qualifications
  - Timetables
- Copy of most recent SEN record and summary (e.g. percentage at each stage, area of need)
- Most recent provision maps (e.g. whole school, key stage, examples of individual maps)
- Summary and analysis of attainment and progress:
  - Tracking information
  - National Curriculum assessment data
  - Target setting summary

- Other progress data, including reading ages
- Monitoring and evaluation evidence, e.g.
  - Monitoring plan and timetable
  - Evaluations of the impact of interventions
  - Summary of observations, work scrutiny, discussions with pupils, etc.
  - Evidence of parental feedback of satisfaction with SEN provision
  - Evaluations of impact of any outside services (e.g. health, educational psychologists)
- Continuing professional development for all staff and its impact, e.g.
  - Record of CPD provided for all staff
  - Record of CPD for SEN team
  - Evidence of impact of CPD on provision and progress
- SEN budget information, e.g.
  - Budget allocations and amount spent
  - Pupil Premium spend
- Minutes of SEN meetings, e.g.
  - Whole school/SEN team
  - Governors
  - Parents
- Governors' report to parents (SEN information)

The inspection visit

Before the inspection

▓ Discuss with the head teacher if there are any particular issues the inspectors are likely to explore (e.g. where the data is showing underachievement). Gather evidence of action taken on these particular issues.

▓ Pre-empt challenging questions by having a rationale for every aspect of provision (e.g. 'We tried that but it didn't work so now we are trying ... and will evaluate it at the end of term' or 'We've identified a professional development need in staff on ASD so we are providing ...').

▓ Remind all staff of their responsibilities regarding pupils with SEN and the importance of having a clear understanding of their needs and how to support individuals.

▓ Check that all support staff have a clear understanding of their roles. Remember, for a lesson observation to be judged outstanding, support staff must be working in partnership with teachers to have a positive impact on pupil progress.

During the inspection

▓ Make sure all staff are well briefed on key points, such as what inspectors will be looking for in lessons with regards to SEN.

▓ Be ready for your meeting with the inspector and take your evidence files with examples of success, showing evidence of excellent pupil progress and positive feedback from pupils and parents. Take any prepared case studies with you and use them as examples of success. If the inspector comments on something for which you're unprepared, be honest, but give the impression that it will be addressed as soon as possible.

▣ Keep calm and remember that you are the professional showing a job well done – you need to sell yourself!

After the inspection

▣ Consider aspects for improvement and revisit your improvement or action plan to ensure you have them covered.

▣ Make sure you and your team learn as much as possible from the feedback given.

▣ When the visit is over, celebrate your successes, go home and enjoy a well-deserved treat!

In brief

1. Be well prepared in order to show inspectors what you're doing, how and why you're doing it, what's working well and how you plan to make any necessary improvements.

2. As part of whole-school self-evaluation, the SENCO needs to gather evidence to show the effectiveness of SEN provision and to evaluate how well the school

helps the most vulnerable children make good and outstanding progress.

3. You will need to collect a range of evidence from data analysis, lesson observations, scrutiny of work and discussions with pupils, parents and staff.

4. Gather evidence for case studies of particular pupils which will help you to tell their 'story'.

5. The evidence collected will enable you to make an evaluation against each of the four key judgements of the Ofsted framework.

Conclusion

Do you remember the brief job description at the start of the book? Having now outlined some of the major roles of the SENCO, I'm sure you'll agree that there are many more skills and areas of knowledge that could be added. The job of the SENCO can be never-ending: the more you do, the more you find to do, so you need to be able to prioritise. The quick checklist at the end of this chapter provides an overview of some of the key actions to help you do this.

Managing your time

In Chapter 1, some of the key challenges for SENCOs were outlined. This book has aimed to address some of those challenges and provide ideas for practical solutions. Another issue, however, that always comes high on any SENCO's list of concerns is that of time – or lack of it! So let's take a look at some final top tips from a very experienced SENCO on how to effectively manage your time.

Top tips

Gareth Morewood, director of curriculum support (SENCO) at Priestnall School in Stockport, suggests the following strategies:

- Allow yourself dedicated time to do the different aspects of the job, including paperwork and making phone calls. Allocate specific periods/time-slots and stick to them.
- Ensure you discuss the need for time with your head teacher.
- Develop the skills within your team and, where possible, delegate elements of your day-to-day role.
- Make sure SEN is recognised as a shared responsibility and make time to train staff as part of a school-wide approach.
- Have a clear line of communication to the head teacher to ensure that whole-school ethos and leadership decisions support your vision.
- Don't feel like you should know all the answers – you can't be an expert in every area of SEN! Keep a list of key contacts, phone numbers or websites where you can find further information or signpost others.
- Develop a solutions-focused outlook that takes an imaginative approach to the use of time and resources.

- Keep the SENCO-mantra in the forefront of your mind: 'big impact – small effort'. Try to make sure you find solutions that have the most impact, but don't require weeks of preparation to deliver.
- Remember to make time for yourself – you need to retain a work–life balance or you'll burn yourself out.

For further useful guidance and support on managing the SENCO role, take a look at Gareth's website at www. gdmorewood.com/

So, does the 'Perfect SENCO' exist? Well, in reality, nobody is perfect. But if we can confidently say that progress and achievement for pupils with SEN in our schools is outstanding, then that is perhaps as near to perfection as we could ever wish for.

The perfect SENCO:
quick checklist of key actions

- ▣ Keep up to date with the changes happening in SEN and the Ofsted framework. ☑
- ▣ Develop a SEN action plan that links with whole-school priorities. ☑
- ▣ Review the SEN policy with parents and governors, when appropriate. ☑
- ▣ Clarify school criteria for identifying SEN. ☑
- ▣ Check staff are making reasonable adjustments for disabled pupils. ☑
- ▣ Prioritise high quality, inclusive teaching. ☑
- ▣ Support staff to remove barriers to access, participation and learning. ☑
- ▣ Use provision mapping as a way of coordinating, monitoring and evaluating whole-school provision. ☑
- ▣ Develop a clear overview of the SEN budget and spend. ☑
- ▣ Use a range of data to evidence attainment, progress and achievement of pupils with SEN. ☑

- Model high expectations for all pupils, including those with SEN. ☑
- Provide a range of CPD opportunities for staff. ☑
- Monitor the effectiveness of TA deployment. ☑
- Consider my own professional development needs. ☑
- Set clear expectations and systems of communication for partnership working. ☑
- Place parents and pupils at the heart of decision-making processes. ☑
- Work with my SEN governor. ☑
- Gather evidence to show the overall effectiveness of SEN provision and impact on pupil progress. ☑

References and further reading

Beere, J. (2012). *The Perfect Ofsted Lesson*. Carmarthen: Crown House Publishing.

Bennathan, M. and Boxall, M. (2013). *The Boxall Profile Handbook (Revised)*. London: Nurture Group Network.

Blatchford, P., Bassett, P., Brown, P., Martin, C., Russell, A. and Webster, R. (2009). *The Deployment and Impact of Support Staff Project*. Research Brief: DCSF-RB148. London: DCSF. Available at: http://www.ioe.ac.uk/diss_research_summary.pdf (accessed 17 June 2013).

Brookes, G. (2013). *What Works Well For Children and Young People with Literacy Difficulties? The Effectiveness of Intervention Schemes*, 4th edn. Bracknell: Dyslexia-SpLD Trust. Available at: http://oneeducation.co.uk/download/file/What_works_for_children_fourth_ed.pdf (accessed 17 June 2013).

Cheminais, R. (2010). *Rita Cheminais' Handbook for SENCOs*. London: Sage Publications.

CUREE (2005). *National Framework for Coaching and Mentoring*. London: DCFS. Available at: http://www.curee-paccts.com/resources/publications/national-framework-mentoring-and-coaching (accessed 17 June 2013).

DCSF (2009). *Achievement for All: Guidance for Schools*. Available at: dera.ioe.ac.uk/2401/1/sen_afa_guide_00782.pdf (accessed 17 June 2013).

DfE (2001). *Special Educational Needs: Code of Practice*. Available at: http://www.education.gov.uk/aboutdfe/statutory/g00213170/special-educational-needs-code-of-practice (accessed 17 June 2013).

DfE (2009). The Education (Special Educational Needs Co-ordinators) (England) (Amendment) Regulations 2009. SI 2009/1387. Available at: http://www.legislation.gov.uk/uksi/2009/1387/made?view=plain (accessed 17 June 2013).

DfE (2010). *Progression 2010–11: Advice on Improving Data to Raise Attainment and Maximise the Progress of Learners with Special Educational Needs*. Available at: http://webarchive.nationalarchives.gov. uk/20110809101133/ http://nsonline.org.uk/node/437685 (accessed 1 July 2013).

DfE (2011). *Support and Aspiration: A New Approach to Special Educational Needs and Disability. A Consultation*. Available at: http://webarchive. nationalarchives.gov.uk/20130401151715/ https://www.education.gov.uk/ publications/standard/publicationDetail/Page1/CM%208027 (accessed 17 June 2013).

DfE (2012a). Provision Mapping. Available at: http://www.education.gov. uk/schools/pupilsupport/inclusionandlearnersupport/onetoonetuition/ a00199972/provision-mapping (accessed 17 June 2013).

DfE (2012b). *Support and Aspiration: A New Approach to Special Educational Needs and Disability. Progress and Next Steps*. Available at: http://media. education.gov.uk/assets/files/pdf/s/support%20and%20aspiration%20 a%20new%20approach%20to%20special%20educational%20needs%20 and%20disability%20%20%20progress%20and%20next%20steps.pdf (accessed 17 June 2013).

DfE (2012c). *Teachers' Standards*. Available at: https://www.education.gov. uk/publications/eOrderingDownload/teachers%20standards.pdf (accessed 17 June 2013).

DfE (2013a). The Education (Special Educational Needs Co-ordinator) (England) Regulations 2014. Available at: http://media.education.gov. uk/assets/files/pdf/c/clause%2062%20draft%20regulations%20sen%20 coordinators.pdf (accessed 17 June 2013).

DfE (2013b). Inclusion Development Programme. Available at: http:// www.idponline.org.uk/ (accessed 17 June 2013).

DfE (2013c). *Indicative Draft: The (0–25) Special Educational Needs Code of Practice*. Available at: http://media.education.gov.uk/assets/files/pdf/s/ sen%20code%20of%20practice%20indicative%20draft%20for%20 committee.pdf (accessed 17 June 2013).

DfEE (2000). *The National Literacy Strategy: Grammar for Writing*. DCSF: 0107-2000. Available at: http://webarchive.nationalarchives.gov. uk/20100612050234/nationalstrategies.standards.dcsf.gov.uk/ node/153924 (accessed 17 June 2013).

References and further reading

DfES (2001), Education (Special Educational Needs) (England) (Consolidation) Regulations. SI 2001/3455. Available at http://www.legislation.gov.uk/uksi/2001/3455/contents/made (accessed 1 July 2013).

Education Standards Research Team (2012). *Literacy and Numeracy Catch-Up Strategies*. London: DfE. Available at: http://media.education.gov.uk/assets/files/pdf/l/literacy%20and%20numeracy%20catch%20up%20strategies%20in%20secondary%20schools%2027%20nov%202012.pdf (accessed 17 June 2013).

EHRC (2010). *Education Providers: Schools Guidance*. Available at: http://www.equalityhumanrights.com/advice-and-guidance/education-providers-schools-guidance/ (accessed 17 June 2013).

Great Britain (1995). Disability Discrimination Act 1995. Available at: http://www.legislation.gov.uk/ukpga/1995/50/contents (accessed 17 June 2013).

Great Britain (2010). Equality Act 2010. Available at: http://www.legislation.gov.uk/ukpga/2010/15/contents (accessed 17 June 2013).

Gross, G. (2013). *Beating Bureaucracy in Special Educational Needs*. London: Routledge/Nasen.

Higgins, S., Katsipataki, M., Kokotsaki, D., Coleman, R., Major, L. E. and Coe, R. (2013). *The Sutton Trust-Education Endowment Foundation Teaching and Learning Toolkit*. London: Education Endowment Foundation. Available at: http://educationendowmentfoundation.org.uk/toolkit/about-the-toolkit/ (accessed 17 June 2013).

House of Commons (2012). Children and Families Bill 2012–13 to 2013–14. Available at: http://services.parliament.uk/bills/2012-13/childrenandfamilies.html (accessed 17 June 2013).

Lamb, B. (2009). *Special Educational Needs and Parental Confidence: The Lamb Enquiry*. Nottingham: DCSF. Available at: http://webarchive.nationalarchives.gov.uk/20130401151715/https://www.education.gov.uk/publications/eOrderingDownload/01143-2009DOM-EN.pdf (accessed 17 June 2013).

Martin, J. (2012). *Making and Measuring Progress for Pupils with SEND: Strategies to Achieve and Demonstrate Progress* [ebook]. London: Optimus Education. Available from http://www.optimus-education.com/shop/making-and-measuring-progress-pupils-send-strategies-achieve-and-demonstrate-progress-ebook/

Nasen (2012). A Whole School Approach to Improving Access, Participation and Achievement. Available at: http://www.nasentraining. org.uk/resources/ (accessed 17 June 2013).

Ofsted (2010). *A Statement Is Not Enough: Ofsted Review of Special Educational Needs and Disability*. Available at: http://www.ofsted.gov.uk/ news/statement-not-enough-ofsted-review-of-special-educational-needs-and-disability-0 (accessed 17 June 2013).

Ofsted (2012), *The Evaluation Schedule for the Inspection of Maintained Schools and Academies*. Ref: 090098. London: Ofsted.

Ofsted (2013a). *The Framework for School Inspection* 2012. Ref: 120100. Available at: http://www.ofsted.gov.uk/resources/framework-for-school-inspection (accessed 17 June 2013).

Ofsted (2013b). *School Inspection Handbook*. Ref: 120101. Available at: http://www.ofsted.gov.uk/resources/school-inspection-handbook (accessed 17 June 2013).

Ofsted (2013c). *Subsidiary Guidance: Supporting the Inspection of Maintained Schools and Academies*. Ref: 110166. Available at: http://www.ofsted.gov. uk/resources/subsidiary-guidance-supporting-inspection-of-maintained-schools-and-academies (accessed 17 June 2013).

Packer, N. (2012). 'Providing CPD through Collaborative In-House Approaches', *Special Children Magazine* 210: 19–20.

Webster, R. and Blatchford, P. (2013). *Making a Statement Project: Final Report*. London: Institute of Education. Available at: http://www. schoolsupportstaff.net/mastreport.pdf (accessed 17 June 2013).